First published in Great Britain in 2021 by
Academy Press, 23 College Road, Brighton BN2 1JB

ISBN 978-0-9558923-4-9

Front Cover: Statue of Antonius at the top of long walk
Back Cover: Statue of The Lion and the Horse

Designed by Academy Press
Artwork by The Graphics Room
Printing by Hobs Reading

For further copies enquire
from Academy Press
jemimaschlee@gmail.com

The statues at Rousham Park

By Ann Schlee

ap Academy Press

Introduction

No one ever bought a statue lightly. They are too expensive and too heavy for that. The eighteenth-century landowners who decorated their newly landscaped gardens with classical statuary may have seen versions of the same figures in the great public and private collections visited on the Grand Tour, but only the very wealthy could afford to bring such bulky trophies home with them. The others bought copies, cast or carved, from the leading sculpture yards on the outskirts of London, such as those of the Scheemakers brothers at Millbank, the Cheere brothers at Hyde Park Corner and the Coadestone works at Lambeth.

Italian sculptor Antonio Canova in his studio with Henry Thresham, by Hugh Douglas Hamilton.
© V&A Picture Library

They chose with care and when these purchases had made their slow journey by barge and then by farm cart along narrow country lanes, they placed them deliberately. The designer of the garden might choose a statue to close a vista, draw attention to a view, decorate a wall or fountain or to create a pleasurable surprise at a turn in the path. The landowner, however much he and the designer worked in sympathy, might have made his choice for more complex and more personal reasons. Although it is impossible to know with any certainty what these might have been, the attempt to trace their various associations is revealing of how these men hoped to divert and perhaps impress their visitors and what they might want of their garden as a private retreat.

Mostly they purchased copies of statues that were, in their turn, Roman versions of long-vanished Greek originals. Implicit in them were stories from Graeco/Roman mythology, instantly recognizable to their classically educated owners and their visitors, so that what might be seen as the simple narrative of a tour around the grounds ('… and then we reach the temple … and then we glimpse the lake …') would be pleasurably interrupted with other, more adventurous narratives lodged in the mind since childhood.

More than that, to such minds, trained in the rich metaphoric language of myth, statues prompt cryptic interpretations. The presence of a *Hercules* at the entrance to a garden suggests that it is under his mighty protection. At a fork in a path the same figure can turn the choice of route into a matter of moral decision, especially if one way leads upward and the other down. The presence of *Venus* on the one hand and Hadrian's lover, *Antinous*, on the other, can be interpreted as a choice of sexual proclivities. A recumbent nymph in a cave can make it into a place of poetic inspiration or, if a river god, into a scene of dynastic prophesy reminiscent of Virgil's *Aeneid*. A *Pegasus* striking his hoof on a stony outcrop transforms it into Mount

Helicon and proclaims the garden to be a home to all the muses. More obviously, niches may be occupied by busts of Shakespeare, Alfred the Great and Merlin which can suggest political persuasions of a sturdy Britishness at odds with Franco-Catholic sympathies or the German origins of the reigning monarch. Through his choice of statues the mind of the garden's owner half expresses, half conceals itself.

Statues can do more than that. They draw a landscape into relation with the human form. They remain there, mysteriously, when night falls. To walk round a landscape is to render it plastic. The shapes in front of you alter and rearrange themselves with every step. Statues with their fixed posture and their stony gaze see it differently. It is instinct, when they are set in a landscape, to seek them out; to stand beside them and attempt to see what they see. Immediately, what lies ahead goes still. They establish a place when the living passers-by destabilize it. Coming from an ancient past, they appear to halt the passage of time. To the cyclical time of plants and the linear time of the history of the place is added time suspended.

The Owner

One of the many landowners who renovated their gardens in the first half of the eighteenth century was James Dormer, a bachelor and a soldier who, at the age of 56, inherited Rousham Park in Oxfordshire in 1737 from his elder brother, Robert. The Dormers were a military family. As the lives of James Dormer's parents and grandparents had been shaped by the vicissitudes of the English Civil Wars, his generation's were shaped by repercussions from the Glorious Revolution and by

This portrait of General James Dormer by JeanBaptiste van Loo, 1738, shows a man alert, but approachable. He has chosen to be painted with one hand resting on a book. His hand is covering the title on the spine so that it might represent no book in particular or all books. Courtesy of a private collection

VANLOO

the War of the Spanish Succession.

His career to date had been colourful and marked by bereavement. In his mid-twenties he had served with distinction under Marlborough at Blenheim, where he was severely wounded and his brother, Philip, killed. Later another brother, Charles, was killed at Almanzo.

Battle of Blenheim, by Joshua Ross jr. © Alamy stock photo

James survived to fight again at Ramillies and at Saragossa. He was imprisoned at Briheuga and later sent a gift of 200 poundsworth of books to a convent where the nuns had shown him kindness at that time. In 1725, after service in England during the Jacobite unrest, he was sent to Lisbon as envoy extraordinary.

There Dormer's career suffered a setback when he entered into an unseemly feud with Thomas Burnett, the British consul. The account of the fracas which he sent to a cousin, Stephen Cottrell, shows traces of a lingering excitement but little, if any, remorse.

> '[Burnett] has given out that I was to be recalled in disgrace. In short, I have been constantly kept on the fret. I said to one who told him again, he would provoke me to order my servants to beat him ... He threw out slighting words upon my threats and never went out in his chaise without a case of pistols. The servants, by my orders, went to take him out of the chaise and beat him ... Twas so difficult to get him out, that before my servants could do it, his footmen were upon them with drawn swords. When mine drew it was unfortunately happened that one of them run him in the calf of the leg, and another cut him on the back of his hand' (Gordon 1999, cited by Mowl 2007, p. 238).

Whatever the truth of the consul's original slander, Dormer was now recalled to London, with his diplomatic career at an end. Despite this, his fortunes in the army continued to prosper. Over the next three years, concurrent with the urgent programme of renovation at Rousham, Dormer was successively made major general, lieutenant general and appointed Governor of Hull (*ODNB* 2004). He has been described, in these later years, as 'a violent, self-indulgent old bachelor soldier' (Mowl 2007, p. 239), which may be true, in part. Something of his impulsive vigour can be glimpsed in a letter from Alexander Pope to the Earl of Oxford written on

15 August 1731: 'I am away to Lord Cobham's at a single day's warning. I was transported hither by the impetuous spirit of the Brigadier Dormer and am to be hurryd back by a reflux of the same violent tide in two days.'

It seems likely, however, from his family background and his interests, that General Dormer's character was more complex. His mother's family, the Cottrells, held the hereditary post of master of ceremonies and translator to Charles I, Charles II and James II, which suggests that some degree of artistry and a care for words ran in that side of the family. His maternal grandfather, Sir Charles Cottrell, was said by Samuel Pepys to be 'ingenious' and by an Italian friend to be 'of kind disposition, soft and gentle, assiduous in his visits, of wise counsel, exemplary life style, and the best conversation.'

Anne Dormer, the general's mother, was a cultivated woman, unusually literate for her age. In the course of a copious correspondence with her sister, she describes herself as having a 'soft nature' (Dormer, fol. 176r, as cited in *ODNB* 2004), inclined to a 'naturall bashfulness' (*ibid.*, fol. 205r) and as having to struggle with melancholy all her life'. Her brother, Charles Lodowick Cottrell (the general's uncle) seems to have lost a similar struggle. His son was to write of him that, at the end of a troubled and dissolute life, 'his melancholy continues and sometimes increases he turns everything that's said as a reflection upon him'. Some of the familial melancholy lingers at Rousham, even on its most benign days. For some tastes at least, it is most beautiful in autumn.

Although James Dormer's father died when he was 10, his mother lived until James was 16 and may well have been the first to instil in him a love of books and 'that strong prejudice which we [i.e. men of his class and era] so early and so deeply feel in favour of everything that relates to Roman and Greek antiquity' (Spence's

Merton College, Oxford University, by David Loggan, 1675. © Welcome Images

Anecdotes, as cited by Jourdain 1948, p. 75). Dormer pursued his classical education at Merton College, Oxford, where a Cottrell uncle was Master, and was remembered there as being 'withal a curious[1] gentleman, and well-skilled in books' (Nichols, as cited by Coffin 1986). Cicero and Chaucer were said to be among his favourite authors. Later he assembled an extensive library, remarkably large for his times, of mainly classical and French literature and books of prints (Gordon 1999, p. 106; Müller 1997, p.179). (Its sale after his death lasted twenty days and took up some

[1] Shorter Oxford English Dictionary examples from the eighteenth century support meanings of: 1. careful, solicitous, accurate, skilful; 2. desirous of seeing or knowing, inquisitive; 3. skilled as a connoisseur or virtuoso.

three thousand lots.) He also became a passionate collector of bronzes. It would have been these interests that drew him into membership of the gifted, sophisticated circle of the Kit-Cat Club in London,[2] where his elder brother, Colonel Robert, was already a member and a friend of Swift, Gay and Pope. However congenial James Dormer might have hoped to find the company of these cultivated men, by then he had lived long in the boisterous, bawdy, occasionally brutal world of soldiering, hunting and politics. If he retained any shadow of a gentle melancholy and sensitivity inherited

[2] The Kit-Cat Club had its origins in the 1690s when Jacob Tonson, a bookseller, grown prosperous on his sales of Milton and Dryden, invited aspiring writers to weekly feasts of mutton pies and wine at the Cat and Fiddle tavern in Gray's Inn Lane. These excellent pies, known as 'kit-cats' after the pastry chef, Christopher Cat, gave the club its name. Although primarily devoted to the arts, the club had strong affiliations to the Whig party. It attracted such leading literary figures as Addison, Steele, Congreve and Vanbrugh as well as politicians, soldiers, painters and Whig grandees.

from his mother, he would have learned to keep it well masked. Too well masked perhaps, or perhaps it was his seriousness which led to his never being entirely accepted by his brother's London friends, even to have been a butt for their wit. There is mild mockery in the Hon. George Berkeley's letter of 1734 to Lady Suffolk:

> 'We set out yesterday, two coachfuls of us, from Rousham. Stowe is in great beauty, the master [i.e. Lord Cobham] is in excellent spirits, by which the Major General [James Dormer] gets a new tormentor; not that his old one (Pope) was not sufficient, who had really laughed himself fat at poor Jemmy's expense, who in proportion has fretted himself lean' (Suffolk, vol. 2, p. 49).

In 1734 he writes again, with sharper malice, from Shotover:

> 'We performed our journey here with great ease, only little Pope was very ill the whole day; and compassion for him may pass for a reason why I was so little entertained with a very lively conversation which would have been very agreable to me, as would the misfortunes which were very happily contrived for the Major General [Dormer] during the whole journey. We shall set out this morning for Rousham' (*ibid.*, p. 49).

On his brother Robert's death Dormer had also acquired the hereditary post of colonel of the Grenadier Horse Guards and three other estates in Oxfordshire and Buckinghamshire. Of all of these it was Rousham Park, a Jacobean manor house built by his grandfather, Sir Robert Dormer, in 1635, where the general decided to settle and to make it his own by adding a library for his books and by supplying the only element which Rousham lacked to make it a seat fitting for a gentleman of taste and learning: a collection of classical sculpture.

The Statuaries

It was a fortunate time to begin such a collection. By the middle of the century, a number of artist-craftsmen who had emigrated from the Low Countries in the wake of William of Orange's accession were becoming established in London and, over the next decade, rose to dominate the English market in garden statuary. Jan Van Nost the elder, whose name became anglicized to John Nost, was first known to have been working in England in 1606 when Vertue refers to him as 'foreman' to the Antwerp-born sculptor Arnold Quellin (Vertue, vol. 4, p. 35). When Quellin died in that same year, Nost married his widow and sole heir,[3] thereby acquiring much of Quellin's work.

By the end of the century, Nost owned three properties and commanded prices as high as £600 for a marble monument. His chief business, however, was the production of lead statuary for country estates all over England in response to the demand stimulated by the Grand Tour. He sold copies of some of the most famous statues in Rome, most notably the Farnese *Hercules* and the *Venus de Medici*, as well as a wide range of fauns and satyrs. Nost died a wealthy man in 1710 and left the business to his nephew, who, in the year before Dormer's accession to Rousham, sold it (with the Hyde Park iron yard and workshop) to **John Cheere** (1709–87), a Londoner of Huguenot descent. Cheere's elder brother, Henry, was already established as one of the leading sculptors and stonecutters in London, his only competitors being two more Flemish emigrés, Michael Rysbeck and Peter Scheemakers. With the assistance of his brother, John Cheere developed his new acquisition into a highly productive source of lead and plaster casts. His Hyde Park Corner yard, which became one of

[3] Frances, the daughter of the topographical painter Jan Sibrechts.

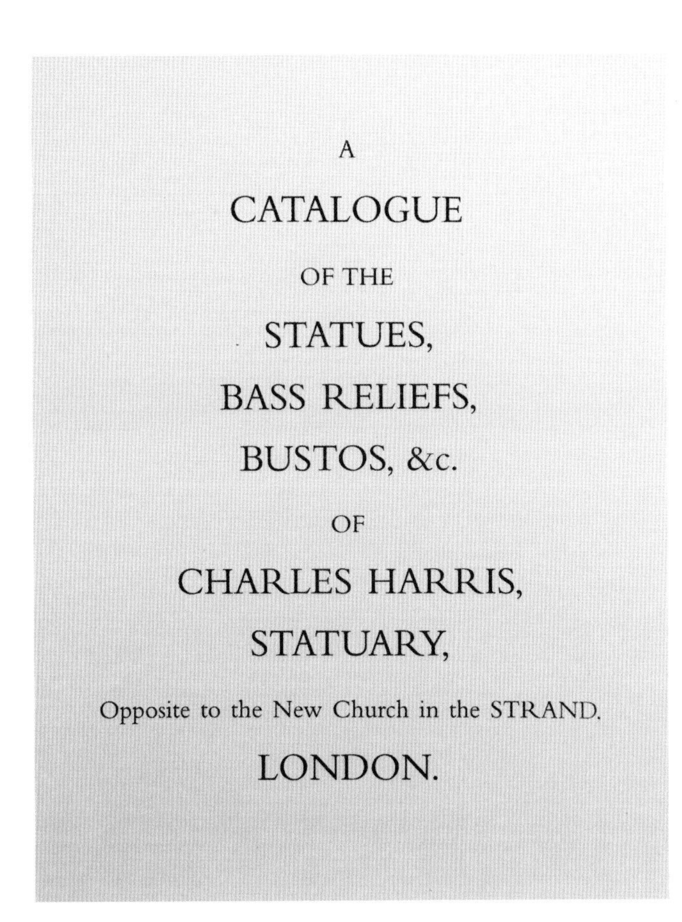

A

CATALOGUE

OF THE

STATUES,

BASS RELIEFS,

BUSTOS, &c.

OF

CHARLES HARRIS,

STATUARY,

Opposite to the New Church in the STRAND.

LONDON.

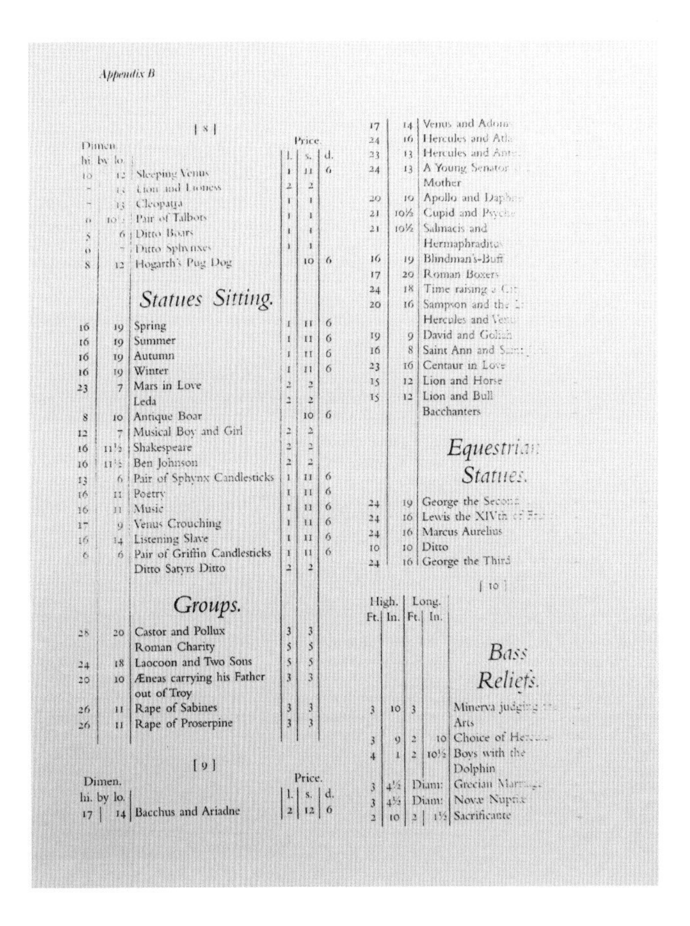

Appendix B

[8]

Dimen. hi.	by lo.		Price l.	s.	d.
10	12	Sleeping Venus	1	11	6
[illegible]	13	Lion and Lioness	2	2	
[illegible]	13	Cleopatra	1	1	
6	10½	Pair of Talbots	1	1	
5	6	Ditto Boars	1	1	
6	7	Ditto Sphynxes	1	1	
8	12	Hogarth's Pug Dog		10	6
		Statues Sitting.			
16	19	Spring	1	11	6
16	19	Summer	1	11	6
16	19	Autumn	1	11	6
16	19	Winter	1	11	6
23	7	Mars in Love	2	2	
		Leda	2	2	
8	10	Antique Boar		10	6
12	7	Musical Boy and Girl	2	2	
16	11½	Shakespeare	2	2	
16	11½	Ben Johnson	2	2	
13	6	Pair of Sphynx Candlesticks	1	11	6
16	11	Poetry	1	11	6
16	11	Music	1	11	6
17	9	Venus Crouching	1	11	6
16	14	Listening Slave	1	11	6
6	6	Pair of Griffin Candlesticks	1	11	6
		Ditto Satyrs Ditto	2	2	
		Groups.			
28	20	Castor and Pollux	3	3	
		Roman Charity	5	5	
24	18	Laocoon and Two Sons	5	5	
20	10	Æneas carrying his Father out of Troy	3	3	
26	11	Rape of Sabines	3	3	
26	11	Rape of Proserpine	3	3	

[9]

Dimen. hi.	by lo.		Price l.	s.	d.
17	14	Bacchus and Ariadne	2	12	6
17	14	Venus and Adon			
24	16	Hercules and Atl			
23	13	Hercules and Ant			
24	13	A Young Senator … Mother			
20	10	Apollo and Daph			
21	10½	Cupid and Psych			
21	10½	Salmacis and Hermaphrodit			
16	19	Blindman's-Buff			
17	20	Roman Boxers			
24	18	Time raising a C			
20	16	Sampson and the			
		Hercules and Ven			
19	9	David and Goliah			
16	8	Saint Ann and S			
23	16	Centaur in Love			
15	12	Lion and Horse			
15	12	Lion and Bull			
		Bacchanters			
		Equestrian Statues.			
24	19	George the Second			
24	16	Lewis the XIVth of Fr			
24	16	Marcus Aurelius			
10	10	Ditto			
24	16	George the Third			

[10]

High. Ft.	In.	Long. Ft.	In.	
				Bass Reliefs.
3	10	3		Minerva judging the Arts
3	9	2	10	Choice of Her
4	1	2	10½	Boys with the Dolphin
3	4½	Diam:		Grecian Marr
3	4½	Diam:		Novæ Nuptiæ
2	10	2	1½	Sacrificante

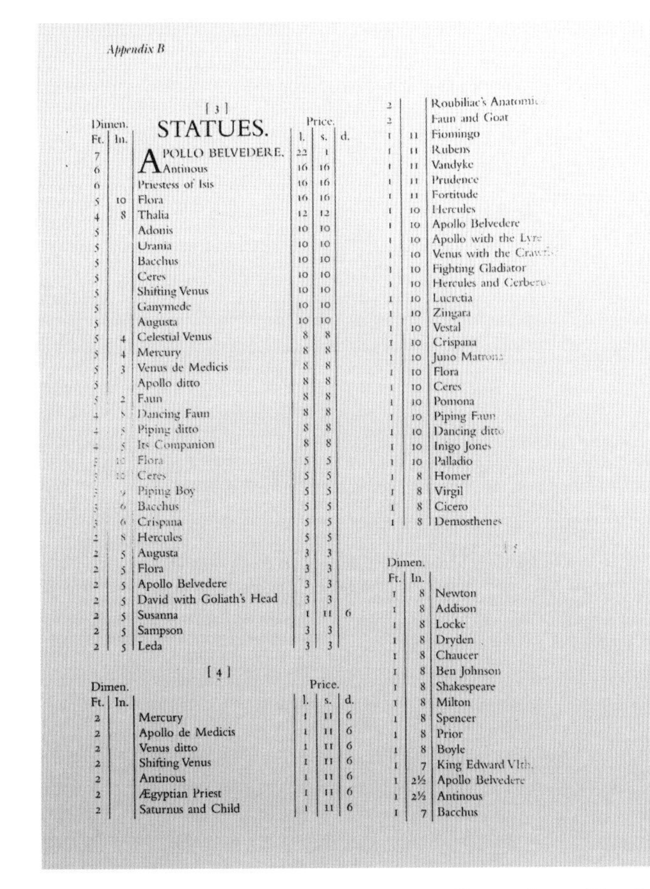

Appendix B

[3]

STATUES.

Dimen. Ft.	In.		Price l.	s.	d.
7		APOLLO BELVEDERE.	22	1	
6		Antinous	16	16	
6		Priestess of Isis	16	16	
5	10	Flora	16	16	
4	8	Thalia	12	12	
5		Adonis	10	10	
5		Urania	10	10	
5		Bacchus	10	10	
5		Ceres	10	10	
5		Shifting Venus	10	10	
5		Ganymede	10	10	
5		Augusta	10	10	
5	4	Celestial Venus	8	8	
5	4	Mercury	8	8	
5	3	Venus de Medicis	8	8	
5		Apollo ditto	8	8	
5	2	Faun	8	8	
4	8	Dancing Faun	8	8	
4	5	Piping ditto	8	8	
4	5	Its Companion	8	8	
3	10	Flora	5	5	
3	10	Ceres	5	5	
3	9	Piping Boy	5	5	
3	6	Bacchus	5	5	
3	6	Crispana	5	5	
2	8	Hercules	5	5	
2	5	Augusta	3	3	
2	5	Flora	3	3	
2	5	Apollo Belvedere	3	3	
2	5	David with Goliath's Head	3	3	
2	5	Susanna	1	11	6
2	5	Sampson	3	3	
2	5	Leda	3	3	

[4]

Dimen. Ft.	In.		Price l.	s.	d.
2		Mercury	1	11	6
2		Apollo de Medicis	1	11	6
2		Venus ditto	1	11	6
2		Shifting Venus	1	11	6
2		Antinous	1	11	6
2		Ægyptian Priest	1	11	6
2		Saturnus and Child	1	11	6
2		Roubiliac's Anatomi			
2		Faun and Goat			
1	11	Fiomingo			
1	11	Rubens			
1	11	Vandyke			
1	11	Prudence			
1	11	Fortitude			
1	10	Hercules			
1	10	Apollo Belvedere			
1	10	Apollo with the Lyre			
1	10	Venus with the Craw			
1	10	Fighting Gladiator			
1	10	Hercules and Cerberus			
1	10	Lucretia			
1	10	Zingara			
1	10	Vestal			
1	10	Crispana			
1	10	Juno Matrona			
1	10	Flora			
1	10	Ceres			
1	10	Pomona			
1	10	Piping Faun			
1	10	Dancing ditto			
1	10	Inigo Jones			
1	10	Palladio			
1	8	Homer			
1	8	Virgil			
1	8	Cicero			
1	8	Demosthenes			

[5]

Dimen. Ft.	In.	
1	8	Newton
1	8	Addison
1	8	Locke
1	8	Dryden
1	8	Chaucer
1	8	Ben Johnson
1	8	Shakespeare
1	8	Milton
1	8	Spencer
1	8	Prior
1	8	Boyle
1	7	King Edward VIth.
1	2½	Apollo Belvedere
1	2½	Antinous
1	7	Bacchus

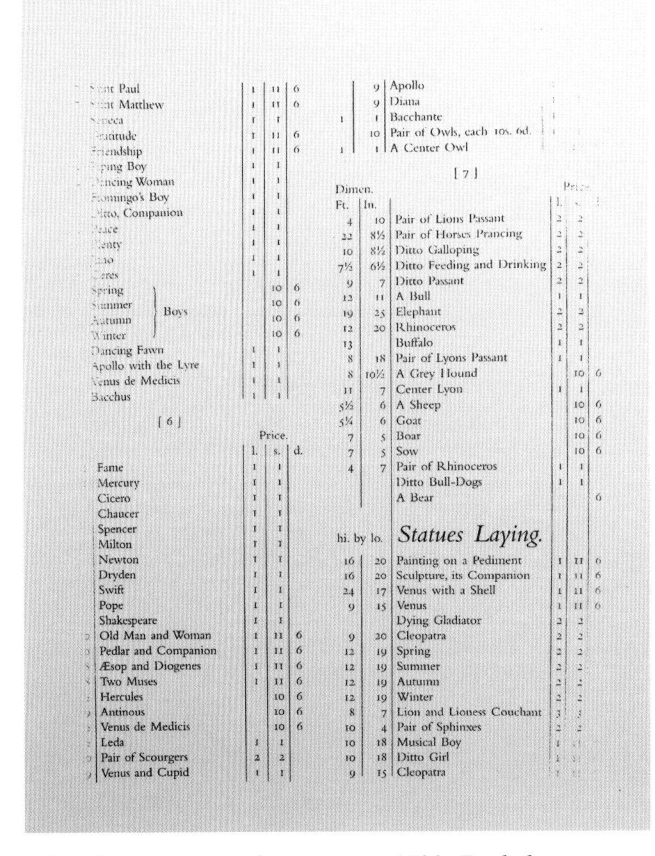

	l.	s.	d.
Saint Paul	1	11	6
Saint Matthew	1	11	6
Seneca	1	1	
Gratitude	1	11	6
Friendship	1	11	6
Piping Boy	1	1	
Dancing Woman	1	1	
Fiomingo's Boy	1	1	
Ditto, Companion	1	1	
Peace	1	1	
Plenty	1	1	
Juno	1	1	
Ceres	1	1	
Spring (Boys)		10	6
Summer (Boys)		10	6
Autumn (Boys)		10	6
Winter (Boys)		10	6
Dancing Fawn	1	1	
Apollo with the Lyre	1	1	
Venus de Medicis	1	1	
Bacchus	1	1	

[6]

Dimen. Ft.	In.		Price l.	s.	d.
		Fame	1	1	
		Mercury	1	1	
		Cicero	1	1	
		Chaucer	1	1	
		Spencer	1	1	
		Milton	1	1	
		Newton	1	1	
		Dryden	1	1	
		Swift	1	1	
		Pope	1	1	
		Shakespeare	1	1	
		Old Man and Woman	1	11	6
		Pedlar and Companion	1	11	6
		Æsop and Diogenes	1	11	6
		Two Muses	1	11	6
		Hercules		10	6
		Antinous		10	6
		Venus de Medicis		10	6
		Leda	1	1	
		Pair of Scourgers	2	2	
		Venus and Cupid	1	1	
	9	Apollo			
	9	Diana			
1	1	Bacchante			
	10	Pair of Owls, each 10s. 6d.			
1	1	A Center Owl			

[7]

Dimen. Ft.	In.		Price l.	s.	d.
4	10	Pair of Lions Passant	2	2	
22	8½	Pair of Horses Prancing	2	2	
10	8½	Ditto Galloping	2	2	
7½	6½	Ditto Feeding and Drinking	2	2	
9	7	Ditto Passant	2	2	
12	11	A Bull	1	1	
19	25	Elephant	2	2	
12	20	Rhinoceros	2	2	
13		Buffalo	1	1	
8	18	Pair of Lyons Passant	1	1	
8	10½	A Grey Hound		10	6
11	7	Center Lyon	1	1	
5½	6	A Sheep		10	6
5¼	6	Goat		10	6
7	5	Boar		10	6
7	5	Sow		10	6
4	7	Pair of Rhinoceros	1	1	
		Ditto Bull-Dogs	1	1	
		A Bear			6
hi.	by lo.	*Statues Laying.*			
16	20	Painting on a Pediment	1	11	6
16	20	Sculpture, its Companion	1	11	6
24	17	Venus with a Shell	1	11	6
9	15	Venus	1	11	6
		Dying Gladiator	2	2	
9	20	Cleopatra	2	2	
12	19	Spring	2	2	
12	19	Summer	2	2	
12	19	Autumn	2	2	
12	19	Winter	2	2	
8	7	Lion and Lioness Couchant	3	3	
10	4	Pair of Sphinxes	2	2	
10	18	Musical Boy	1	[illegible]	
10	18	Ditto Girl	1	[illegible]	
9	15	Cleopatra	1	[illegible]	

Pages from Charles Harris's sales catalogue of statuary, c. 1790, English version. Courtesy of Victoria & Albert Museum, London

BUSTES *grands comme Nature,*

A Deux Guinées chaque.

Socrate
Inigo Jones
Paladio
Cromwell
Homére
Ciceron
Horace
Virgile
Platon
Adrien
Mithridate
Galba
Demosthene
Alfred, Roi d'Angleterre
L'Apollon de Belvedere
Antinous
Caracalla
Geta
Machiavel
Dante
Petrarque
Boccacio
Marc Auréle
Sénéque
Sylla
Enobarbe
Jule Cæsar
Brutus
Pompée
Bacchus
Agrippine
Faustine

Flore
Venus de Medicis
Julie
Sapphon
Laocoon
Le grand Chancelier Bacon
Le Chevalier Isaac Newton
Shakespeare
Dryden
Le Comte de Halifax
Le Lords { Ligonier, Chesterfield, Chatham, Camden }
BECKFORD, celebre Lord Mayre de Londres.
SWIFT, le fameux Doyen de St. Patrice
C. Townsend
Handel
Frewin, Mead, Hervey { Illustres médecins }
Garrick
Le Chevalier Fielding, Commissaire distingué
L'Esclave qui écoute
Pope
Paul Whitehead, Poete

Ciceron - - -	1	11	6
Seneque - - -	1	11	6

BUSTES de *Vingt-quatre Pouces,*

A Un Livre Six Chelins chaque.

Titus
Anacreòn
La Magona Carthaginoiſe
Brutus
Ariſtote
Epicure
Seneque
Socrate
Demoſthene
Ciceron
Homer
Horace
Virgil
Germanicus
Marc Aurele
Milon
Minerve
Julie
La Suſanne
Une Veſtable
La Zingare
Niobé
La même
Fauſtine
Plantille
Inigo Jones

Palladio
Chaucer
Milton, l'auteur du Paradis Perdu
Le grand Chancelier Bacon
Le Chevalier Iſaac Newton
Shakeſpeare, le 1er poëte dramatique
Ben Johnſon, grand poëte comique
Spencer, fameux poëte allegorique
Locke, auteur de l'Eſſai ſur l'Entendement Humain
Dryden, poëte fameux
Addiſon
Prior, l'Horace Anglais
Pope
Hervey }
Mead } M. D.
Sydenham }
Garrick
Sterne
Ciceron
Horace

Le Roy Guillaume III	1	11	6
Le Roy Alfred	1	11	6

Pages from the French edition of Charles Harris's catalogue courtesy of the Department of Rare Books and Manuscripts at the Yale Center for British Art.

the sights of London, was described by a contemporary visitor:

> 'I came out at the lodge and stepped into Mr. Cheere's yard which, on account of the numberless figures in stone, lead and plaster you would sware was in a country fair or market, made up of spruce squires, haymakers with rakes in their hands, shepherds and shepherdesses, bagpipes and pipes and fiddlers, Dutch skippers and English sailors enough to supply a first-rate man-of-war' (anon., cited by Gunnis 1934, p. 90).

In 1761, an Irish clergyman described another part of the yard as '... an Assembly of Gods and Goddesses, Juno, Minerva, Venus de Medici, Jupiter, Mars, Neptune and rural Deities Pan and frisking Satyrs, with an Infinite Multitude of Meer Dancers, Haymakers, Gladiators, Wrestlers, Huntsmen, and Fowlers' (BL, Add. MS275951).

In the frontispiece to his book *The Analysis of Beauty* (1753), William Hogarth depicts what is thought to be Cheere's sculpture yard, showing some of his famous models crowded together with open sketchbooks, hoists, studies of faces and a single discarded boot. An illustration of a later date by Thomas Rowlandson depicts an unnamed sculpture yard where a row of classical busts look down from the rear wall on an animated scene of mythological figures and prospective buyers. Rowlandson is keen to suggest the mixed interests such places aroused: customers ogle the statues and the statues ogle one another. Demand in the first half of the eighteenth century was high; the business prospered and proved the contemporary quip that that the London statuaries had learned the art of turning lead into gold.

In the same decade that saw that saw this upward turn in John Cheere's fortunes, the Antwerp-born sculptor **Peter Scheemakers** (1691–1781) grew impatient with the slow advance of his own. He had worked in London since at least 1720 without the success he had hoped for. Fashions had moved away from the continental baroque

Frontispiece to William Hogarth's 'Analysis of Beauty', possibly showing John Cheere's studio, 1753.
© Alamy stock photo (detail)

style in which he had been trained in Holland, but he was quick to see that the rising wealth and aspiration of both the Whig gentry and city merchants had opened up a new market of buyers who saw in Republican Rome a fitting model for the England of their generation and political persuasions: 'a perfect state free of the horrors of Popery' (Roscoe 1999). Scheemakers saw in the fact that his chief rival, Michael Rysbeck, had never been to Italy a chance to get the advantage of him. Being a man of great industry and with a shrewd business sense, he sold up the entire stock from his yard at Millbank and, with the proceeds, he and his business partner Laurent Delvaux set out for Rome.

There, between 1728 and 1730, the two men worked ceaselessly, studying the city's sculptural masterpieces. As well as filling at least four sketchbooks with drawings, Scheemakers made twenty or more terracotta models of the most famous works in the great Roman collections. George Vertue wrote of these on their arrival in London, 'I am perswaded no one master herettofore has brought back so many compleate works in that perfection of their own studies into England …' (Vertue, vol. 3, pp. 44–45).

Delvaux stayed on in Rome, but Scheemakers returned to London and re-opened the Millbank yard. The Roman models, which he was later to sculpt, on commission, in Portland stone or marble were, as he had hoped, to provide the basis for his future reputation among the newly affluent middle class: '… their betters might dominate the market in antiquities but they, in their local communities, could prove their gentility by commissioning sculpture from the foremost available classicist' (Roscoe 1999). He too became a wealthy man. It is a measure of the attendant rise in social status to which a successful statuary might aspire that whereas John Nost, at the height of his career, was referred to as 'one of the best hands in England', less than

Previous pages: 'A Statuary's Yard', by Thomas Rowlandson. © Alamy stock photo

a century later, Henry Cheere, John Cheere's brother, became a knight (1761) and within another five years was made baronet.

The expansion of these two businesses, Cheere's and Scheemakers', led to a great increase in the number and quality of sculptures available at affordable prices. Almost all the statues at Rousham came from one or other of them.

The Garden Designers

Some renovation of Rousham was already under way when the general acceded. From 1720, Colonel Robert had employed **Charles Bridgeman**, royal gardener to George II and Queen Caroline,[4] to design a 'new garden' on land recently acquired on the northern boundary of his property: a shallow valley sloping down to the river's edge, which came to be known as the Vale of Venus. It was Bridgeman who first addressed the two particular challenges that the site presented: its relative smallness and the need to unite the old garden with the new. He met the first problem by extending visitors' impressions of the garden to include the countryside beyond its actual limits. To the west, he employed the 'simple enchantment' (Walpole as cited

[4] Bridgeman was in charge of the gardens at Hampton Court, St James's Park, Windsor, Hyde Park and Kensington Gardens where he created the Round Pond and the Serpentine.

Portrait of Charles Bridgeman, attributed to William Hogarth. Vancouver Gallery.
© Alamy stock photo

by Willis, pp. 18–19) of a curved ha-ha, an innovation to disguise the boundary. To the north, with the co-operation of neighbouring landowners, Bridgeman (and later Kent) contrived to draw the fields on the farther bank of the Cherwell visually within the bounds of the Dormer estate. Trees were 'tipped' and a mill in the middle distance was given a medieval facade by Kent, who also designed a fake ruin of three gothic arches to form an 'eye catcher' on the horizon. The steep banks below the Bowling Green, originally five descending, terraced parterres, and the narrow neck of land between the old and new gardens were 'smoothed' into concave slopes so that nothing might interfere with the sweep of the eye to the land on the far side of the river. By these sleights of vision the whole estate was given an illusory extent and antiquity.[5]

[5] As there is no mention of either of these features in the reports on renovations after 1738, it is presumed that they were in place by then and were at least planned by Bridgeman.

'The Temple of the Mill and Eye Catcher', by William Kent. Courtesy of a private collection

'The Temple of the Mill and the Mill Wheel, Rousham', by William Kent. Courtesy of Graduate Center (Decorative Arts, Design History, Material Culture), New York. Photographer: Bruce White. © The Devonshire Collection, Chatsworth. Reproduced by permission of Chatsworth Settlement Trustees

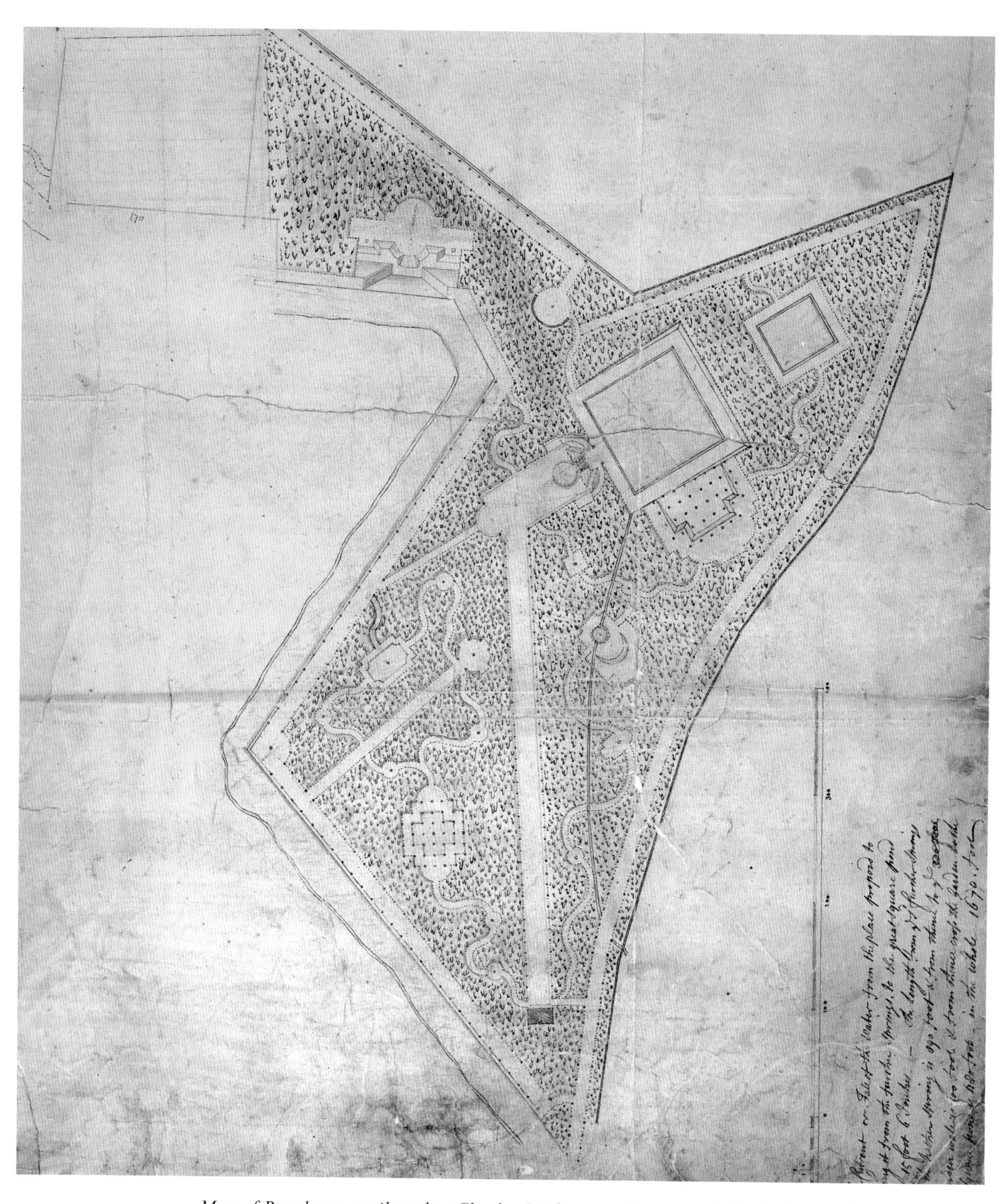

Map of Rousham, attributed to Charles Bridgeman. Courtesy of the Oxford Bodleian Library

Within the Dormer property, Bridgeman concentrated his efforts on the recently acquired area, now known as the Vale of Venus. What is believed to be a reconstructive plan of his work, dating from 1720, shows a mixture of formal and more 'natural' elements. A square and an octagonal pond are aligned with one another and meet a straight avenue of elm trees at what is nearly a right angle. These geometric shapes are interspersed with irregular patches of wilderness penetrated by serpentine walks: for all its partial formality, Bridgeman's plan shows considerable sympathy with the site by building on Rousham's most admired natural advantages: its plentiful supply of running water and the views that the garden commands of the countryside on the far side of the river.

Two sites are indicated as intended water displays: the Vale and the small woodland clearing by the Cherwell still known as Bridgeman's Theatre. There are also two viewing points of the scene on the opposite bank: one at the north end of the Bowling Green and the other from the narrow neck of land leading to the Vale. These developments found favour in Colonel Robert's day. Alexander Pope, who had shown ingenuity in making the most of his own 'three inches' of garden on the Thames at Twickenham, visited Rousham in 1728 and described it in a letter to his friend Martha Blount as 'the prettiest place for waterfalls, jetts, ponds enclosed with

beautiful scenes of green and hanging wood, that ever I saw' (Pope to Martha Blount, 4 September 1728, as cited by Gordon 1999, p. 34). The Hon. George Berkeley, writing to Mrs Henrietta Howard in 1734, confessed a partiality for Rousham over the far grander and more celebrated Stowe: 'One advantage must be allowed it; there is at the bottom of a sloping hill … a most delightful stream' (as cited by Willis, p. 67). It is noticeable that neither writer makes any mention of sculpture in their letters and that Bridgeman indicates only one possible site for a statue in his plan; that is, above the square pond at the head of the Vale.

Bridgeman died in the year that James Dormer inherited. Without delay, the general employed William Kent, a friend and another Kit-Cat member, to carry on the work of making both house and garden his own. Kent was by then at the height of his career. Four years earlier Sir Thomas Robinson had written to Lord Carlisle:

> 'There is a new taste in gardening just arisen, which has been practiced with so great success at the Prince's garden in Town,[6] that a general alteration of some of the most considerable gardens in the Kingdom is begun, after Mr. Kent's notion of gardening, viz. to lay them out and work without level or line' (HMC 1897, p. 143).

Dormer had chosen fashionably, but he had also chosen well. Kent was uniquely placed to give expression to his employer's love of the classics within the context of this very English setting. He had a natural sympathy for landscape. Horace Walpole was to recognize the sensuous and very tactile elements in this: 'He felt the delicious contrast of hill and valley changing imperceptibly into one another, tasted the beauty of the gentle swell or concave scoop …' (Walpole as cited in Chase 1943). As well as being an architect and a painter, Kent, in his own way, was a sculptor, able to approach landscape as if it were a pliant substance.

Moreover, owner and designer complemented each other in a very important way. The general seems never to have been on the Grand Tour.[7] His knowledge of classical and Italian sculpture appears to have come from his own library and from viewing other, wealthier men's collections in England. Kent was able to bring to Rousham his own enchanted vision of a classical Arcadia, formed over ten years of

[6] Charlton House, acquired by Frederick Prince of Wales in 1733.

[7] There is no reference to him in Ingamells' dictionary of 'Grand Tourists'.

Portrait of William Kent, c. 1710. © Alamy stock photo

travel in Italy. He had been no idle 'Grand Tourist': at the age of 24 his travels had been financed by a consortium of Yorkshire gentlemen as a necessary part of his training to become a painter of dramatic scenes from classical and biblical history. His patrons must also have intended that, as his skill developed, he would become useful to them by copying old masters in oils and by acting as a reliable agent on the continent for the purchase of paintings, drawings, and sculpture.

Kent was young and poorly educated when he set out, but he travelled with men of knowledge and refinement and was bound to be influenced by their tastes and interests. His original companions were Daniel Lock, an architect, and John Talman, an architect's son who had come to sketch buildings in Rome with a view to reviving his father's failing London practice. As he travelled in their company, architecture claimed more and more of Kent's attention. In 1709 he was in Rome, still studying painting under an Italian master but finding time to spend every Thursday with Talman 'seeing fine palaces'. Sculpture played an integral part in the design of these, both in their architecture and in the gardens adjoining them.

Talman returned to England but Kent continued to study painting in Rome under the patronage of successive and increasingly wealthy men. In 1714 he met the 17-year-old Thomas Coke who paid his expenses on a trip they shared to the north of Italy. Kent's widening of interest was reflected by the fact that he titled his manuscript journal of that expedition 'Remarks by way of Painting and Archt.'. It was on his return to Rome that Kent met his most famous patron, Lord Burlington, and was soon engaged in purchasing paintings and statues for both Burlington and Coke as well as pressing on with his own interests. In November 1718 he wrote that he was 'continualy a drawing ornements & archetecture, & getting things yt I think will be neciseary for me in England' [sic]. By December he was 'makeing all preperations

I can to come for England next spring.' He worked with the urgency of knowing that the rich resources of Italy would soon be beyond his reach: '... [spending] what little mony I have in prints & stucco figures as heads & feet etc which will be of great use to me when I cannot see ye antiques' (Blackett-Ord 2001, pp. 101–102).

When he did eventually return to England in November 1719, he brought away with him books of sketches and a mind stored with visual reference, later to be reinforced in Lord Burlington's library at Chiswick. His illustrations for Virgil's

'A Peaceful Country', by Inigo Jones (1573–1652). Design for scene 2 of Sir William Davenport's masque 'Salmacide Spoiia', 1640. © The Devonshire Collections, Chatsworth. Reproduced by permission of Chatsworth Settlement Trustees.

Aeneid and Spencer's *The Faerie Queene* and his study of Inigo Jones' masque scenery provided further experience in creating landscape settings for human figures. Nearly twenty years later, with his own distinctive style fully developed, Kent brought all these accumulated factors into play at Rousham and found there a wealth of raw material to work on: cliff, river, ponds, meadow, woods – all in miniature.

James Dormer was a more tactful inheritor than many of his generation, content to keep his renovations within the bounds of family tradition. He preserved most of the interior of the old house as it had been in his father's and grandfather's day, including the original oak door with musket holes bored by Sir Robert so that he could gun down any attacking Roundheads during the Civil Wars. Kent extended the Jacobean house by adding matching Palladian wings to the east and west: that to the west was to house the general's library. His approach was one of synthesis: drawing in the latest fashions in architecture and gardening without destroying the old. In the garden, although it is difficult to distinguish exactly where Kent took over and Bridgeman left off, it would seem that Kent developed further the five sites his predecessor had identified but softened the geometric shapes shown on the earlier plan. All five sites were to become settings for sculpture.

Work was begun immediately with full awareness of the difficulties involved: the distance from suppliers, the vagaries of weather and Kent's commitments to other clients. Over the next four years he seems only to have found time to visit Rousham once a year, while the general, despite his eager and exacting interest in the renovations, spent most of the winter in his London house in Berkeley Street. He therefore engaged as overseer during his absences in London a man he knew well and could trust to understand and carry out his wishes: William White, who had been actively involved in the Burnett fracas and who was the only member of the general's former entourage in Lisbon to be recalled with him.

White seems to have been installed at Rousham even before James inherited. Frances Cottrell-Dormer mentions him as one of the hastily assembled witnesses to Robert Dormer's will. She refers to him as 'Mr. William White of Rousham' and adds, 'This person appears to have been some steward or upper servant deeply in the confidence of Colonel and General Dormer' (Cottrell-Dormer 2012, p. 52). As her words suggest, White's presence there and the lack of clarity about his exact social status within the household were the cause of some discomfort and correspondence between the brothers' titled, lady visitors. A letter written by the Duchess of Queensberry to the Countess of Suffolk shows the 'steward' neatly side-stepping the issue of whether to dress as servant or equal when included in a shooting party at Chilgrove by appearing in 'a Portugese habit'.

Communication between these four men – White and Clary[8] at Rousham and Kent and the general in London – was a continuing problem, but with the fortunate outcome that the resulting correspondence between White and Dormer gives a weekly account of the progress of the renovations during the general's absences. This, combined with a long letter from Clary, recommending the beauties of Rousham to the general's heirs and giving a detailed picture of the garden in its completed form in 1750, means that the creation of Rousham is unusually well documented.

To avoid confusion, a plan of the garden dated 1739 is believed to have been drawn up by White 'after discussions with Kent [and] incorporating another plan made by the gardener [Clary]' (Batey's introduction to Müller 1997, p. 178). One of its purposes seems to have been to establish exactly where the general wished

[8] Clary's name was originally Macclary. He dropped the 'Mac' from his name, preferring to be known as 'Clary', when he discovered that there had been an important eighteenth-century landowner of that name in his own village of Steeple Aston (Batey 1983, p. 125). He was head gardener at Rousham at this period and he worked closely with White.

the statues and busts to be placed. Thus, in a letter dated June 1739, White writes about the placing of the Antinous:

> 'I find myself even with the gardener's advice under great difficulty in regard to the figure you mention insomuch as I cannot prevail with myself to break up the ground for laying the foundation for the pedestal. Here enclosed goes Clary's draft of the ground by which you will I hope be able to mark out the very spot to your own good liking. I am apt to think the situation marked E upon the plan at the top of the ascent from the Elm Walk would not be altogether amiss. It would there be seen from the building and likewise from Hayford's Bridge, where as should it be erected at the bottom of the ascent from the Elm Walk it will be nowhere in view except in that walk only. The situation determined it will be necessary to direct which way the figure is to face – the walk or the road' (White to Dormer, June 1739, as cited by Müller 1997, p. 184).

Although a comparison of Kent's plan with Bridgeman's shows little alteration in the general layout, it marks ten sites intended for sculpture in comparison to Bridgeman's one and adds four new garden structures: the Palladian Gateway, the Townsend Building, the Pyramid Building and the Praeneste, Kent's name for a seven-arch arcade built into the slope above the right-angled bend in the Cherwell. All of these were designed to contain niches for sculpture. The change made in the appearance of the garden, when all was in place, is recorded by George Vertue who visited Rousham in 1741, after Kent's work was complete. He describes it as now being 'Grand and Noble finely disposd adorned with statues, arcades, Temples …' (Vertue, vol. 4, p. 191). Were this to suggest excess, it would be misleading. No one has ever accused Rousham, as Walpole did Stowe, of being 'over-templed' or over-statued: a tribute to Kent's sensitivity in placing each of these features in the overall landscape.

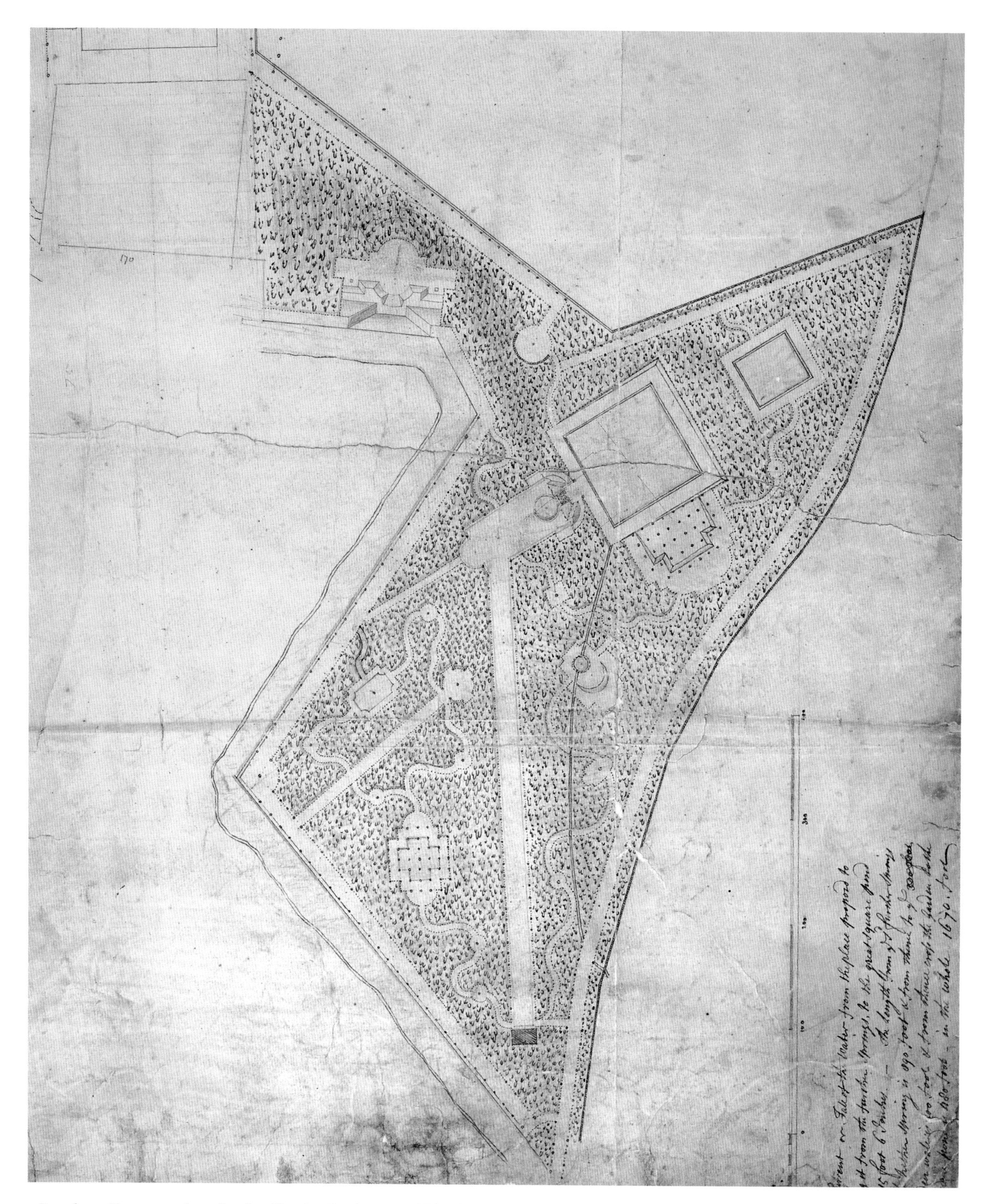

Rousham House garden plan by Charles Bridgeman, 1715–20

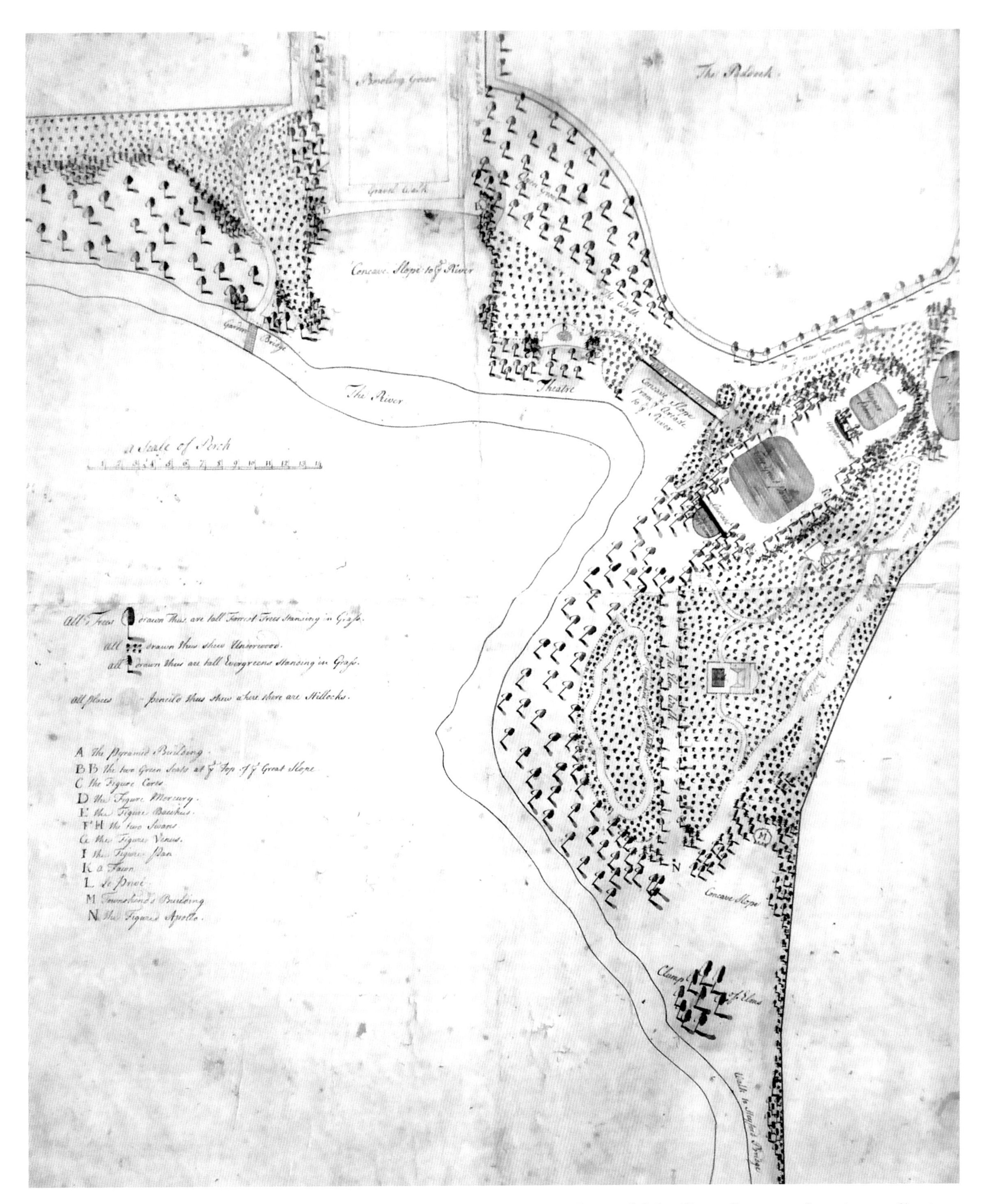

Plan of Rousham Gardens, attributed to William White and John Clary. Courtesy of a private collection

Kent's established method of work was to start each new project by bringing in a large force of labourers to complete any necessary earth shifting before he embarked on the rest of the scheme (Jourdain 1948, p. 77). By the summer of 1738 White was reporting on 'the multiplicity of things now in hand' with between fifty and seventy labourers working simultaneously to widen the river, clear the ponds and create rustic arches over the cascades in the Vale of Venus. In November he reports, 'Some hundred loads of earth are removed and many more still to come away from the terras [of the Praeneste]'. Bridgeman's Theatre, by the river, was to be 'rough levelled'. In other places the ground was raised and built into a 'Mount'.

By the following year work was under way on the Praeneste itself. Work had also begun on the Pyramid Building, a small, single-roomed structure at the most western point of the property. That all these landscaped areas – the Vale of Venus, Bridgeman's Theatre and the Praeneste Arcade – were designed as future sites for sculpture from the very start of the project is shown by Hal Moggridge's survey of 1982. In it he has demonstrated that, despite the apparent rejection of 'line and level', each of these sites, 'including the sculpture and architecture within it, is broadly symmetrical around its own axis' (p. 189). Once in place, each piece of sculpture was to establish these axial lines and contribute to what Moggridge describes as a 'hidden orderliness' underlying Rousham's 'perceived irregularities'.

Similarly, it is clear from White's letters that niches and plinths to receive particular pieces are from the start included in all aspects of Kent's building schemes; for instance on 23 February 1739, White writes,

> 'Here enclosed goes for Mr. Kent supplies a Draught from ye North porch to the extremity of the library, with my compliments. I beg he would forthwith determine where the neches are to be plac'd and at the same time send directions on what manner they are to be finish'd' (letter from White to Dormer, in Müller 1997, p. 182).

The completion of the building must wait on Kent's instructions as to how exactly their resident busts are to be arranged. On 13 March 1739 he writes again to say that 'The Group of Figures, Venus Gladiator, & the Prisner, all came safe, without

the least scratch' (letter from White to Dormer, in Müller 1997, p. 183).

Throughout the spring of 1739, statuary of different sizes was arriving at Rousham and White's letters are much concerned with their care and placing. Between 10 and 15 March 1739, he reports the 'finishing of the Nech in the Pyramid building & setting up ye Hercules[9] therein' (letter from White to Dormer, in Müller 1997, p. 183). In the same month, White informs the general of the arrival of 'Your letter of March ye 13th with Mr. Kent's plan for the neches'. The work can now move forward. In the same letter he goes on to report that 'the two Bustos, of Tully & Alexander, came this morning safe, as did one of the urns. The other has one handle broke off in a fresh place. The opposite handle came asunder where it had been cemented on' (White to Dormer, 15–22 March, in Müller 1997, p. 183).

[9] This seems to refer to a badly damaged miniature statue of Hercules fighting Antaeus.

There were more abstract issues involved in the placing of the statues. The general would have been familiar with Cicero's wryly indignant letter on being sent a carelessly chosen consignment of figures by an agent:

> 'Had they been of Muses, they would at least have been appropriate for my library and would have been in keeping with my interests, but these Bacchantes, where could I ever put them in my house … what good is a statue of Mars to me, the author of peace?' (Cicero 1927, VII, 23, 1–3).

If the message sent out by a statue was a matter of intense concern in Ancient Rome, it was just as much so in eighteenth-century England. In the previous century, the ownership of a collection of antique marbles, collected on the continent, had been the prerogative of royalty and the aristocracy; proof of great wealth, foreign travel, a highly cultivated taste and a classical education. Now, with the growth of a home market in accurate, affordable copies, a collection of the 'same' statues was within reach of the gentry and middle classes, amongst whom a misplaced statue might reveal a regrettable lapse of taste or lack of education. In 1734, James Ralph, after lamenting the poor quality of statues available in England, adds that,

> 'Nothing is more amazing to me, than the ignorance of most of our gentry in the polite arts, and in statuary particularly; which is so flagrant, that in the vast number of statues which are to be seen in the gardens of this nation, it is almost a miracle if you find a good one. Neither are we alone ignorant of the art itself, but even of the use of it too; for there are as few well situated as chosen: and too many have reason to blush both for the figure itself, and the end it was designed to answer … In the first place, therefore, a statue should be good in itself, in the next, it should be erected to advantage; and lastly, it should, in its own nature, be suited to the place' (Ralph 1734, facs. p. 35).

In the same vein, in his New Principles of Gardening, Batty Langley goes into detail:

> 'There is nothing adds so much to the beauty and grandeur of gardens and nothing more disagreeable as when wrongly placed; as Neptune on a terrace walk, mount etc. or Pan, the God of Sheep in a large basin, Canal or Fountain' (Langley 1728, facs. p. 203).

To save his readers such embarrassments, he goes on to list the deities suitable for representation in different parts of the garden, such as 'open lawns and large lakes, woods and groves, canals and basins, fruit gardens and orchards, flower gardens and so forth'. Kent's finished drawing of the Vale of Venus, the largest of the newly developed garden sites, shows him keeping well within Langley's strictures. The drawing shows water from the upper pond cascading through a rustic arch into the basin below. Here it feeds a fountain before plunging down a triple-arched cascade into a second pond with a second fountain. The fountains are framed on either side and at the back by thin glades of deciduous trees, their trunks lopped of lower branches so that the eye can penetrate between them into a receding distance. In the open centre of the glade, Cheere's lead copy of the *Venus de Medici* perches on the higher set of arches, raised above two lesser Arcadian beings: *Pan and a Satyr*. Urns on plinths and swans, startled from their beds of rushes, balance each other at either end of the arch.[10]

Kent presents this group of fountains and statuary as if it were part of the painted backdrop to a scene of sociable activity. The 'cast' consists of 16 diminutive figures, drawn deliberately small to exaggerate the height of the fountains: ladies and gentlemen, come to view the general's improvements, have brought their little

[10] The cupids formerly on their backs have been stolen.

dogs with them for the outing. They stroll in different directions in groups of two, three or four; the dogs scamper beside them. The men point to particular features with their walking sticks; a gardener approaches the pond with bucket and spade, presumably to clear it of weeds. A lady protects her hat from the fountain's spray with an outspread fan. A solitary figure, leaning deliberately on his stick, stomps off to seek seclusion.

The artist sits where we are as we study it, as it were in the centre of the front row of the stalls so that, for the most part, these 'actors' turn their backs on us and walk away. There are no formal paths, but the wide tracks between the glades are clear and the pale forms of statues lure the human wanderers on across the invisible

'The Vale of Venus', by William Kent, 1738–41. © Topfoto stock photo

line between stage floor and backdrop. There they enter a mythical and timeless space where Kent's vision of Arcadia is still accessible to us.

Pan and the Satyr are reminders that there was another side to the classical conception of Arcadia than that of an idyllic harking back to an age of gold: to modern sensibilities there was a darker one. It was also in Arcadia that women gave vent to their deviant passions in the frenzied worship of Bacchus. There, well-born youths were initiated into the bloody encounters of the hunt as preparation for hand-to-hand combat, and there, in the seclusion of Arcady, older men of the same class instructed protegés of their choice in the arts of war and of homoerotic love (Dettiene 1979, passim).

Intentionally or not, all of these pursuits may be alluded to at Rousham. On the capstone of the largest cascade arch is the carved epitaph, anonymous and undated but probably written by Clement Cottrell-Dormer in the early nineteenth century of a favourite otterhound (see Appendix I). It records not only the huntsman's devotion to his hound and zest for hunting but also scenes of what now seem unacceptable cruelty enacted in the Cherwell below, where the otters who raided Dormer's well-stocked fishing were cornered by hounds and speared with long-handled tridents.

Nor does *Venus* alone preside over the Vale. The largest of the Rousham statues (the one over which White took such particular pains in placing) is a colossal male nude, cast in lead and positioned at the top of the straight alley leading into the

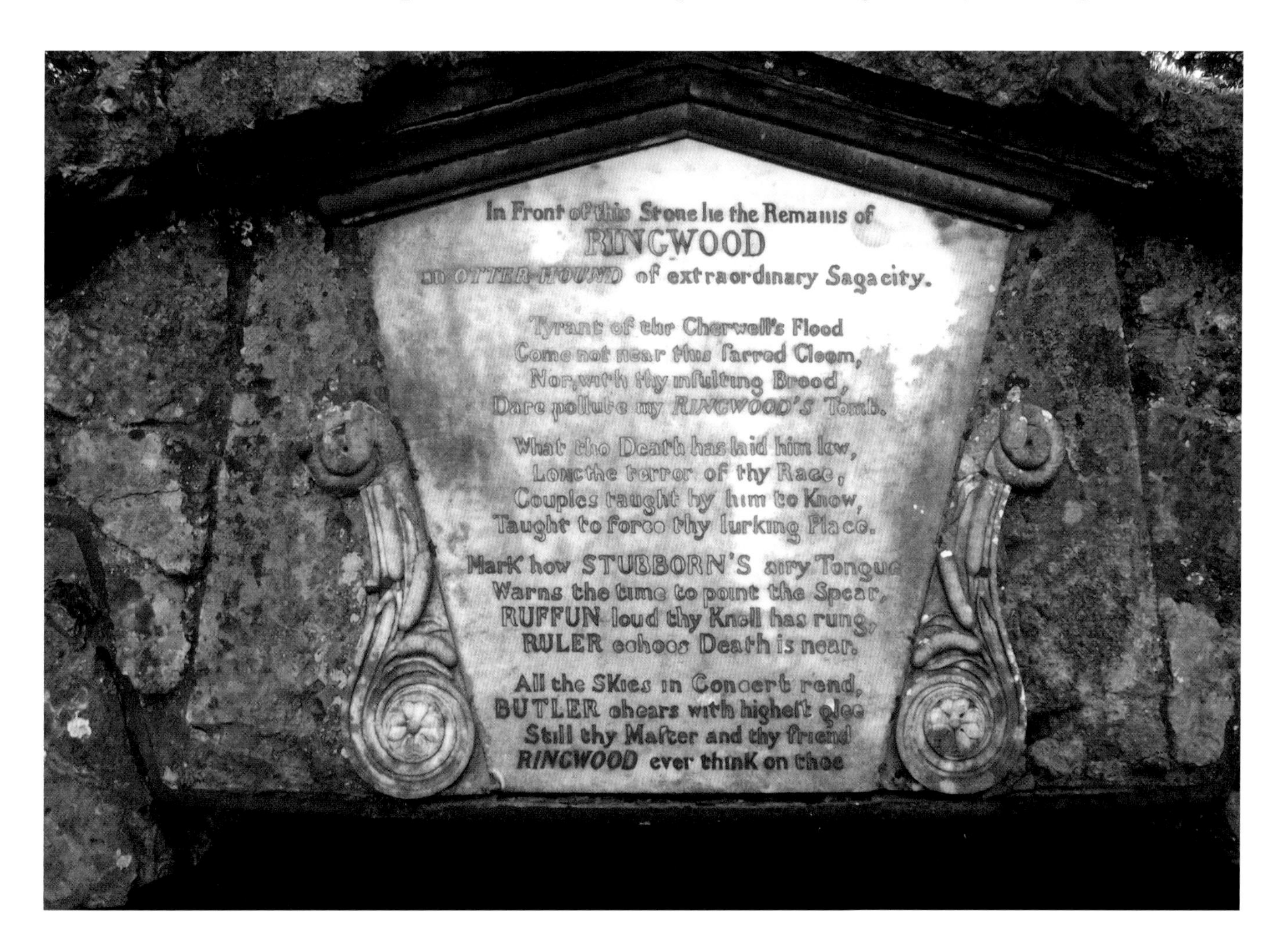

Vale. Although it has been said to represent Apollo, the palm trunk which supports the figure identifies him as the beautiful Greek youth Antinous, Hadrian's hunting companion and his lover, who drowned in the Nile. Cheere's *Antinous* appears, from its stance and the position of the head, to be a version of the Capitoline copy, one of many distributed by Hadrian throughout the Hellenistic world in his campaign to have the youth deified.

The proximity of *Venus and Antinous*, both here and set into niches in Kent's west wing, have been seen as establishing 'Rousham's scheme of paired qualities

and moral choice' (Mowl 2007, p. 237) and hinting at the owner's sexual ambiguity. If Ringwood's epitaph shows an unfeeling zest for blood sports, Antinous' colossal presence near the general's plunge pool may reveal an equal zest for male nudity.

How contemporary viewers reacted to these hints, if hints they be, is impossible to judge: plunge pools of cold water were a fashionable health fad of the day to which the general may well have turned to relieve his gout. However, Horace Walpole, who visited Rousham at least once when he attended the sale of the general's library, read the cultured shorthand easily enough. In The History of the Modern

Taste in Gardening he declared Rousham to be 'as elegant and antique as if the Emperor Julian had selected the most pleasing solitude about Daphne to enjoy a philosophic retirement' (Walpole 1904, p. 65). Walpole can be trusted to be exact in his references. Daphne was a park 5½ miles (9km) south of Antioch, a favourite and somewhat disreputable resort of the townspeople. The Daphne after whom it was named was a nymph of the hunt and wild in her ways (OCCL 1997) while the Emperor Julian, known as 'the apostate', was led by his love of the classical authors to renounce Christianity and return to the pagan gods. Walpole knew exactly where he was in this mesh of cultured allusion.

Today the groves have merged and thickened. The fountains have dried up. The cascades can only be set in motion by the few bold souls who know how to remove a submerged bung from the upper pond. Nevertheless much has been left undisturbed

since Kent completed his work. Antinous is stationed at the top of the ascent so that one comes up behind him and enters the Vale as if in his company. Venus still presides over her romantic chasm. Pan and the Satyr seem only to have moved forward to the edges of this denser woodland to spy on her as she bathes, ready to dart back among the leaves where they can carry on their amorous revels out of sight. The encroaching green gives the impression that Kent's rustic arches and balanced statues stand on the site of an ancient temple ruined and overgrown.

The second site chosen for a water feature (and still known as Bridgeman's Theatre) lies at the centre of Rousham's asymmetric site. In a sketch at the edge of Bridgeman's plan it appears as a long rectangular pond with a fountain playing into a circular basin at its centre. Behind it a tree-covered amphitheatre is cut into the slope of the hill. In front a sharply angled earthwork, in the form of a complicated

series of ramps, leads down to river level. A small square on the flattened summit of each of a pair of flanking pyramids might indicate sites for sculpture.

The slopes and angles in this drawing are more easily read in comparison with another sketch made by Bridgeman of a similar but much larger feature designed for the Duke of Newcastle's pleasure garden at Claremont. That amphitheatre survives, a huge structure covering three acres, and gives some indication of what was intended, on a far smaller scale, for Rousham.

No trace of Bridgeman's Theatre at Rousham remains: indeed it may never have been built. However, a site labelled 'Theatre' appears on a 1738 estate map as a semi-

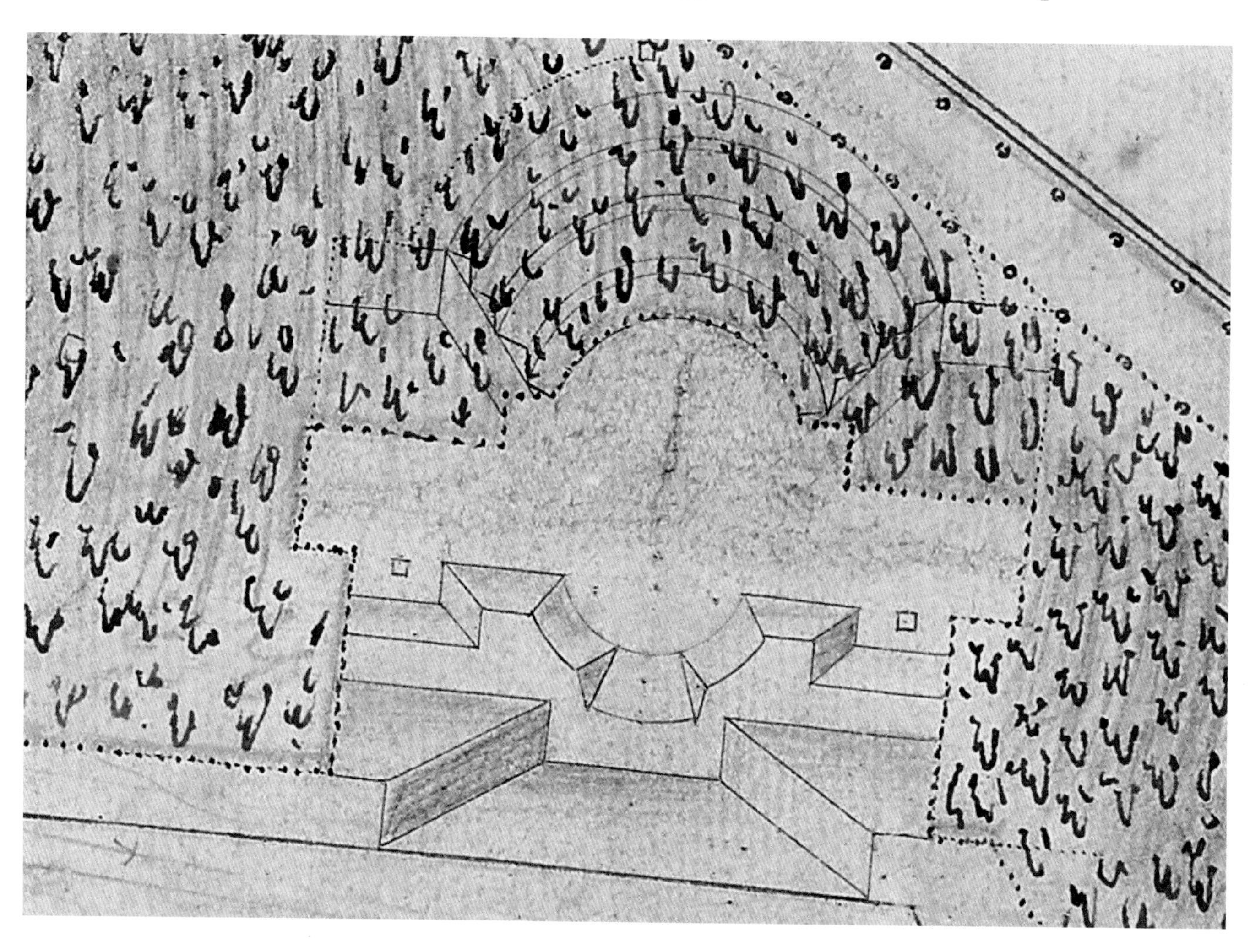

Detail from Bridgeman's plan, showing the Amphitheatre.

'A View of the Amphitheatre at Claremont', by Peter Paul Benazech (1730–98). Royal Collection Trust.
© Her Majesty Queen Elizabeth II 2020

circular clearing in the woods between the Praeneste Arcade and the Grand Slope. In this version the original scheme has been reduced to a fountain in a circular basin. Clary, in his letter of 1750, describes it as it would have been discovered by a visitor:[11]

> 'You turn down a Serpentine Gravel walk, which brings you to a very fine Fountain that plays forty feet high, and falls down among shells, behind it stands a Mercury on a pedestal, backt with a very fine wood, and on one side, stands Bacchus on the other Ceres, upon pedistals, backt with two natural Hillocks,

[11] It was probably the climax of Clary's tour of the garden.

well planted with evergreens ... a little further along the Cherwell makes a natural cascade' (as cited by Batey 1983, p. 130).

In fact the cascade was artificial, made by a low weir, the remnants of which still exist although the wooden garden bridge above it has gone.

Today the spring which fed *Mercury's* fountain has dried up and the shell-lined basin has disappeared but the three statues remain as Clary describes them. Freed of any association with Bridgeman's angular earthwork, they form a tableau similar to that in the Vale. In the centre is Cheere's lead copy of Giambologna's *Mercury*. Balanced on one winged foot, straining after the upraised arm that holds the caduceus, the lithe body is stretched to its utmost limit in readiness for flight. In the original, *Mercury's* weightlessness and detachment from earth is emphasized by his foot being balanced on a waterspout spewed by a Triton. Here, in the Theatre, when seen in conjunction with the upward thrust of the fountain's natural water, he must have appeared already airborne. To the one side *Bacchus* frolics with his panther; to the other *Ceres* stands among stooks of corn and waves the last harvested handful above her head.

There have been frequent finds of statues of these two tutelary deities, Ceres of the grain harvest and Bacchus of the vineyard, near the source of the water supply in excavated Roman gardens. Their presence here at the very heart of Rousham's fecundity carries on that tradition. Below is the river and on the slope above, dry now but still marked by a brick arch, is the site of a spring which provided clean water for the house. Above that is the kitchen garden, the 'destination and climax of the circit' walk (Phibbs 2010). According to Clary's loving description, 'when you enter in, it makes you forget all they Beautys you have seen befor, it looks more like paradice then a kitchen gardn.' He goes on to list its wonders. As well as

fishponds there are 'a pretty many peaches, and nectrons, Great plenty of Apricots, Figgs, Grapes, and Mulberrys, few plumbs, pears, Apples Cherryes, Currents and Goosberries [as well as a] very large handsom Hotthouse, well stockt with very fine pine Apples ...'. And he describes the teeming poultry yard and 'as pretty a set of pigg Stighs, as any is in England' (as cited by Batey 1983, p. 131).

Kent also employed the iconography of Bacchus and Ceres in the small dining salon, now known as the Green Parlour, where the general would have entertained close friends on the garden's produce. His ceiling has as its centrepiece an oval painting showing both deities supporting Venus and Cupid in illustration (according

to Frances Cottrell-Dormer) of a line from Terence: *'Sine Cerere et Baccho frigit Venus'* (Gordon 1999, citing Terence, *The Eunuch*, 4, 732): 'Without food and wine, love grows cold'.

Mercury's presence is consistent with this theme of plentiful provision and hospitality. As the messenger of the gods, plying between Mount Olympus and earth, he came to be seen as the protector of all travellers and of all who followed wandering occupations, including merchants, and particularly corn merchants. As Rome was dependent on imported grain from Egypt to feed her own population, the safety of her merchants was as essential to the avoidance of famine as was the success of the harvest: Ceres and Mercury were closely associated,[12] as would Mercury and Bacchus have been through the wine trade. Together their tableau celebrates Rousham's plenty and hospitality.

Clary describes Bridgeman's Theatre, but he gives no clue as to its function in the garden, nor does any evidence survive, like that of Kent's drawing of the Vale of Venus, to show how the Theatre was intended to be used. Both Pope and Whately[13] see the Theatre's structure as a purely practical means of utilizing a slope between two levels in a garden without altering the natural lay of the land. To Pope it is the 'genius of the place', the mystical, mediating force between the gardener and the natural landscape, which 'scoops in circling theatres the vale' (Pope 1969, lls 58–60). Whately sees it as a 'Natural alternative' to levelling the garden landscape and one which provides varying and extending views of the garden as the viewer climbs to its summit.

Stephen Switzer recommends the theatre as increasing the number of visual experiences to be gained on a single site. He urges that the gardener, instead of

> '... levelling Hills or filling up Dales, ... [should] think it more entertaining [for the visitor] to be sometimes on the Precipice of a Hill viewing all around and under us, and at other times in a Bottom, viewing those goodly Hills and Theatres of Wood or Corn that are above us' (Switzer 1982, vol. II, iii).

Again, comparison with Claremont is helpful. A painting of the amphitheatre from circa 1740 (in a private collection, but reproduced on the back of the National Trust guide brochure) shows three white-painted benches set at different heights

[12] In BCE 495 the first temple of Mercury in Rome was built in the Circus Maximus, not far from the port of Rome and near to the shrine of Ceres.

[13] Thomas Whately (1726–72) was the author of the groundbreaking and influential treatise Observations on Modern Gardening (1770).

and angles, overlooking the lake and Belisle. In an etching of the 1720s (p. 16 of the same brochure), as if to emphasize the theatre's role as a viewing platform, two pale, diminutive figures stand like paired sentinels on the flat-topped pyramids set at either end of the amphitheatre in just the same position as the two squares on the Rousham sketch. Another similar pair are placed centrally at the base of each pyramid. All four look outward across the lake. It is difficult to tell whether they are statues or whether, in a garden otherwise devoid of statuary, they are human visitors:

The Amphitheatre at Claremont. © National Trust Images/Derek Croucher

young men who have found the slopes too challenging to resist. Whether statue or human, they indicate to the viewer one way in which the theatre is intended to be used. In Kent's drawing of the Vale of Venus, the statues seemed to draw visitors to explore deeper into the landscape; here they urge him to climb, be stationary and look outwards.

The term 'theatre' is in itself ambiguous. It refers both to a structure from which action is viewed and to the scene of the action or even the action itself. In whichever sense, where there is a theatre, there is expectation of a spectacle. In the famous gardens of Renaissance Italy (such as those of the Villa Lante, the Villa Aldobrandini, the Vatican and the Villa d'Este, on which Bridgeman's designs for both the Claremont and the Rousham amphitheatres are based), the spectacle is provided by displays of water, the teatro dell'acqua. To ensure sufficient water supplies, whole rivers were diverted at Frascati and Tivoli. At Claremont, where even to fill the lake, water had to be pumped from Esher in elmwood pipes, there was none to spare for fountains and cascades. Instead, the spectacle viewed from the theatre becomes all the human activities the lake inspires. An engraving by Roque of 1754 shows men and women walking, conversing, rowing, punting and fishing. The visitors themselves have become the spectacle and play their parts in a designedly Edenic setting provided by the Duke's menagerie of animals from all over the world and his similar collections of exotic plants and waterfowl. The presence of the amphitheatre invites them to witness and take part in a social drama.

None of these delights is present in the much smaller confines of Rousham but, in the general's day at least, water was relatively plentiful. Even now the faint remains of grassy tiers and the outward-facing statues still invite one to watch the natural theatre created by movement and play of light on the fountain and the cascade

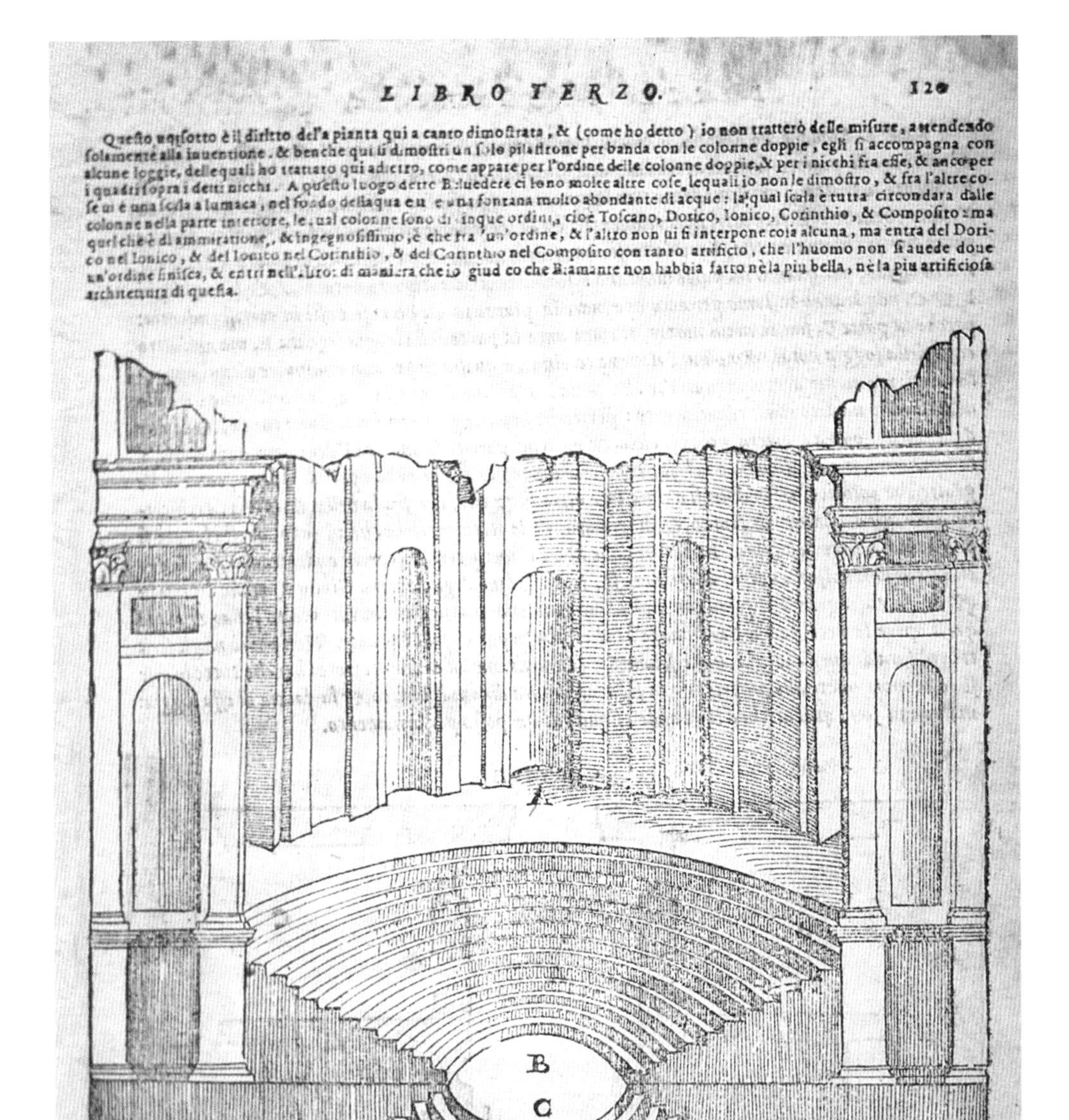

LIBRO TERZO. 120

Questo qui sotto è il diritto della pianta qui a canto dimostrata, & (come ho detto) io non tratterò delle misure, attendendo solamente alla inuentione. & benche qui si dimostri un solo pilastrone per banda con le colonne doppie, egli si accompagna con alcune loggie, dellequali ho trattato qui adietro, come appare per l'ordine delle colonne doppie, & per i nicchi fra esse, & anco per i quadri sopra i detti nicchi. A questo luogo detto Beluedere ci sono molte altre cose, lequali io non le dimostro, & fra l'altre cose ui è una scala a lumaca, nel fondo dellaqua eu e una fontana molto abondante di acque: laqual scala è tutta circondata dalle colonne nella parte interiore, lequal colonne sono di cinque ordini, cioè Toscano, Dorico, Ionico, Corinthio, & Composito: ma quel che è di ammiratione, & ingegnosissimo, è che fra l'un'ordine, & l'altro non ui si interpone cosa alcuna, ma entra del Dorico nel Ionico, & del Ionico nel Corinthio, & del Corinthio nel Composito con tanto artificio, che l'huomo non si auede doue un'ordine finisca, & entri nell'altro: di maniera che io giudico che Bramante non habbia fatto nè la piu bella, nè la piu artificiosa architettura di questa.

The Vatican, Belvedere Court, Bramante's project for the stairs and palace facade.
Courtesy of Cornell University Library

formed by the rush of the Cherwell.

The presence of *Mercury* in Bridgeman's Theatre suggests a third way in which visitors to Rousham were invited to participate in that area of the garden. As the protector of merchants, who traded between one country and another and must do so in a variety of languages, he was also the protector of interpreters and hence of eloquence. Batty Langley recommends as suitable 'for private Cabinets in a Wilderness … representations of Harpocrates God, and Aegerona goddess of Silence, [and] Mercury God of Eloquence' (Langley 1728, facs. p. 205). The apparent contradiction suggests that such secluded woodland groves were considered as suitable retreats, not only for undisturbed thought, but as places where oratory or declamation could be practised in private. Similarly, Pepys tells how he 'went into the gardens … where I played on my flagelette to great advantage' (Pepys 1995, 18 May 1660).

Although there is no evidence of dramatic performance at Rousham, both Pope and Gay were frequent visitors. Certainly in Colonel Robert's day, Pope had a room kept ready for him with bookshelves and a writing desk (Gordon 1999, p. 38). *Mercury's* presence in the Theatre suggests the possibility that on summer visits the company of friends might have withdrawn to Bridgeman's Theatre to hear work written during the day and perhaps take their turns at declaiming favourite passages from the poets, ancient and modern.

The freestanding figures of the Vale and the Theatre speak a common language of association. Their subjects lie outside time in Greek and Roman mythology; their forms are idealized and follow Greek prototypes; their characteristics are abstract. They offer metaphor, even disguise; and so are open to more than one interpretation. By contrast, the portrait busts ordered for Rousham from both Cheere and Scheemakers were of real men and women whose virtues were demonstrated in what were believed to be historical events. Both statuaries ran a very profitable line in busts for display in gardens as well as in libraries: Cheere's cast in plaster and lead and Scheemakers' carved in Portland stone and marble. Scheemakers also made moulds from his more popular models and had them recast in the less costly plaster.

The bust was a distinctly Roman art form. To the Greeks the true depiction of a person must include the body as well as the head. In contrast, the Roman convention of placing busts on herms or columns dehumanizes the body and so lays full emphasis on the face as the true indicator of mind and character. It also, by raising the sculpted face to the same height as the viewer's, creates an illusion of a meeting of minds and exchange of speech.

Whereas the Greeks strove to carve perfect forms, the Romans admired unsparing realism because it was thought that the portrait of a Roman was to be 'his biography, the sum of his experiences, his cursus honorum and Memoria' (Toynbee 1953), hence the preference for busts of men at the end of their public career and as close as possible to death, when further actions for good or ill could no longer intervene to alter the final verdict on their conduct.

The display of such busts in Roman libraries was long established. Writing in the first century CE, Pliny mentioned

> 'a rather new invention ... that of setting up portraits in libraries if not of gold or silver at least of bronze, of those immortal spirits who speak to us in these places; in fact, even portraits of those whose looks were never modelled are made, and our sense of longing gives birth to faces which have not been recorded, as happens to be the case with Homer' (Pliny, XXXV, 9–11).

The practice was widely adopted in Renaissance Italy and across Enlightenment Europe. Classical busts in libraries, on plinths or in the gap in the broken pediments of bookcases are still so much a convention that they go almost unnoticed, the more so now that the ancient faces have grown unfamiliar, their books less widely read, their actions less widely known. But in eighteenth-century England something remained of the belief that, as books give access to the minds of their writers, so their portraits have the power silently to 'speak' at least to those who know what their books contain. Writing in 1714 in *The Spectator* (no. 411), Addison comments that 'A man of a Polite Imagination is let into a great many Pleasures that the Vulgar are not capable of receiving. He can converse with a Picture, and find an agreeable Companion in a Statue.'

Switzer goes further, to claim that statues of famous men can exert good influence:

> 'Statues not only make a magnificent appearance, but tis there also we hieroglyphically read the ideas of valour and renown, that particularly distinguished these ancients above the rest of their fellow creatures and is of continual use and amusement to the serious beholder. Tis there besides [that] the true lineaments of heroism and virtue [are revealed]' (Switzer 1982, pp. 311– 317).

Libraries make an obvious setting for such sculpture but since the time of Plato's academy, gardens too have been considered appropriate places for contemplation and philosophical discussion. One explanation for the many finds of portrait busts in excavated Roman gardens is that, as in Roman libraries so in Roman gardens, busts assumed the living presence of their subjects and served both 'as reflections of the philosophical leanings of their owners and as physical participants in philosophical conversations that would take place near them' (Hartswick 2004, p. 119).

At Rousham, the display of busts in the garden was planned from the beginning of the renovations. As well as designing brackets to display the general's collection of bronzes within the new library and including busts on plinths or columns in the library's decoration, Kent designed matching outdoor niches to hold busts and figures along its north-facing exterior wall and the outer garden wall of the passage joining it to the house. Further niches to contain busts are built into Kent's largest addition to the garden, the Praeneste, a substantial arcade built below the balustrade of the site of the *Dying Gaul* between the Grand Slope and the *Vale of Venus*. The arcade was a structure much used in Italian Renaissance gardens, not only to provide shelter from the sweltering midday sun but to incorporate and display existing vaults from ancient Roman buildings unearthed on the same site. Neither circumstance is likely to apply in England: Pope includes in his mockery of tasteless, spendthrift

improvements those which 'call the wind through long arcades to draw' (Pope 1969, l. 35), However, it seems likely that he would have approved Kent's structure as 'a thing of use'. Even a north-facing arcade like Rousham's can act as a shelter against summer rain and Kent further utilized the Praeneste's diagonal paths to negotiate the steep slope between house and river and its terrace roof as a bridge between the old and new parts of the garden.

The Rousham arcade is a particularly handsome building, composed of seven vaulted Roman arches and originally furnished with sturdy benches, also of Kent's design. Five niches for portrait busts are incorporated into the rear wall. His naming of the arcade after the Roman town, now the modern Palastrina, suggests that Kent based its design on the ancient temple of Jupiter and Fortuna whose massive vaults and terraces survive. Drawings by Palladio and Serglio of imaginary reconstructions show, as well as the simple strength of its arches, flights of paired diagonal steps leading from one level to the other.

Kent's design is perfectly scaled and suited to its function here. Despite its size, it never dominates and within the garden boundaries it can only be seen in its entirety

The remains of Roman baths with modern gardens by Alessandro Donati, Roma vetus ac recens utriusque aedificiis illustrata (1694). Royal Collection Trust.

when approached from the side up one of the diagonal paths. Even then, like the rustic arches in the Vale of Venus, it seems to emerge from a partially excavated landscape, not imposing a decorative scene upon an English landscape but suggesting a ruinous Roman landscape emerging to reveal itself as the basis on which England is built.

By the winter of 1740, busts and statues were arriving at Rousham and White was busy settling them in to both garden and library under instructions from the general in London. As his wording in the letters reveals, he was beginning to think of them in human terms. On 23 November he writes,

'Johnson [a carpenter brought down from London] has removed Caracalla & ye

> Listner[14] into the Arcade. The two bustos of Apollo, & Vespasian are too big to stand in their rooms. The Statue of Apollo since first profferd to ye nech in ye Library has remained there … the new statue arriv'd, shall keep him company' (White to Dormer, 23 November 1740).

On 6 December he writes again that 'Niobe and ye smallest head with whom I am altogether unacquainted travelled as you desir'd to ye Arcade. & Caracalla up again to his corner in the library, where Shackspear faces him' (White to Dormer, 23 November 1740, as cited by Müller 1997, p. 186). This easy interchange between library and arcade indicates that the busts were considered suitable for either setting and suggests that the Praeneste was intended for use as an outdoor library or reading room, providing the general with shelter during the summer months, benches for conversation when he had visitors[15] and, during his solitary hours, the agreeable companionship of his favourite Ancients, provided by busts as well as by books.

Clary lists the portraits, still in the garden in 1750, as Julius Caesar and Calpurnia, Marcus Aurelius and Socrates, Cleopatra, Shakespeare, a Bacchanal, Alexander,[16] a Roman Senator and Niobe.

An expert on the garden has described the collection of busts as 'a soldier's choice'. I suggest that out of the lengthy list of possible purchases offered from Cheere alone, the General would have chosen those he felt would have attributes that reflected his own enthusiasms and beliefs; those he would wish to see around him in his library.

In part these choices do appear military ones, with the inclusion of Julius Caesar and Vespasian, who both did service in Britain. The emperor Caraculla, in common

[14] Müller suggests 'Senator'.

[15] Such as Mr Leigh, the incumbent of Lower Heyford Rectory, a lover of reading and collector of information, whom Dormer called his 'living library' (Cottrell-Dormer 2012, p. 54).

[16] The only survivor of the 1960 thefts, it now stands in a niche on the outer wall of the library

with these two, granted Roman citizenship to all freemen in the Roman Empire. He includes Alexander, the finest general of the ancient world, and Mithradites, Rome's greatest enemy to the East, as models of both military strategy and courage on the battlefield.

There are three women in his selection. Calpurnia, Cleopatra and Niobe. The first two, indeed, have military connections but their associations go beyond these. Calpurnia, Caesar's third wife, whose prescient dream lead her to beg Caesar not to attend the senate on the day of his murder, embodied the ideal of love and faithfulness. Queen Cleopatra, now primarily remembered as the mistress of both Caesar and Anthony, was famed as an expert linguist and conversationalist, characteristics which, that rather than her beauty, Plutarch identified as underpinning her success.

Niobe symbolised grief and bereavement. She lost all of her children at the hands of the gods after boasting that her family was larger than that of the goddess Leto. She wept so inconsolably at their deaths that she was turned into a stone statue. Death and bereavement dominated the General's life beyond the battlefield – it should be remembered that by the time he inherited Rousham he had lost four brothers.

Arguably, Dormer's choice of busts equally reflects his of love classical literature. Cicero, important in late antiquity as a defender of the Republic in the face of tyranny, was a vital conduit for Greek philosophy, and was held up as a model for his rhetorical skills both in his oration and his written prose.

Two other literary choices were Meleager, a Greek poet, and Marcus Aurelius a Roman emperor who followed the Stoic philosophy. Renowned as a philosopher-ruler his twelve books of *Meditations*, written in Greek while on campaign, show him as disillusioned with the world. It is a body of literature that allows for an understanding of the solider as a more complex figure, and perhaps one that reflected

Dormer's own state of mind.

Shakespeare was an essential library companion of the period, whose Roman plays, especially *Julius Caesar* and *Anthony and Cleopatra*, were the main channel through which most English audiences became acquainted with Republican Rome.

He also included a bust of Socrates for whom philosophy, even in its most abstract forms, was embedded in the concerns of life. Conceivably, Dormer shared Socrates's belief that true happiness in a man's life can only be achieved by right living and, like the philosopher, he left no writing himself.

The busts were indeed the choice of a soldier, but a well-read soldier who was no purist. Unlike Cicero. he was content to have a *Bacchanal* in his library; if only in his outdoor one.

Three years earlier Kent had designed a visually similar structure of outdoor niches and busts for Lord Cobham at Stowe. However, in the Temple of British Worthies, each bust was given a Latin caption explaining its inclusion and all were part of an explicit manifesto of Cobham's political views.

Rousham is reticent about its own gathering of the famous. The choice appears to be more personal and to defy the imposition of any rigid scheme, nor is it possible to have a clear impression of the collection as a whole because of thefts of the busts from the Praeneste in the 1960s. It is, however, worth noticing that, as at Stowe and as in the libraries and gardens of the Ancients, the collection demonstrates a balance of men of action and men of intellect. Combined, these attributes make the perfect man: one who enjoys that 'antithetic combination of political [or in the case of James Dormer military] activity and intellectual seclusion noted in the sculpture found in the Villa of the Papiri at Herculaneum' (Hölscher 2004, p. 77).

White's chief concern, as shown in the letters, lies in arranging the statues in

pairs. In the library they were placed to conform with the architecture: thus, on 27 November he writes, 'Sir, The two Great Bustos will stand on each Side the Chimney, for there they stand Square'. They appear to replace another pair, Mithridates and Meleager, who 'are gone to the Arcade' (White to Dormer, 27 November 1740).

In the garden, Kent uses pairs of statues to point up the symmetry of the structures set into the 'natural surroundings'. In some cases this is achieved by pieces that mirror one another, such as the swans at either extreme of *Venus*' arch and the urns at either end of the Arcade. Others are conceived as pairs, either because their subjects have some historical or mythical connection, such as *Bacchus* and *Ceres* in Bridgeman's Theatre and Flora and Plenty in niches on either side of the Palladian Gateway at the public entrance to the garden, or because they form each other's antithesis: Tully[17] the orator and thinker and Alexander the man of action. *Venus* and *Antinous*, the epitomes of feminine and masculine beauty, are placed in identical niches built into the walls flanking the library especially to house them. *Pan*, the god of revelry and excess, and *Hercules*, the semi-divine embodiment of duty obeyed and hardship endured, are placed on matching herms at either end of the balustrade on the Praeneste rooftop terrace.

Where the figures or heads are not originally designed as pairs, White takes great pains that their plinths or herms are adjusted to give them equal height. On 29 November 1739 he writes: 'The Venus is now safe in her Nech next ye house, Antinous likewise in his place … The plinth wanted to be diminished, which Pearson has done about a Straw's bredth & no more …'. In a letter dated 10–15 March 1739, White reports that a brass Apollo has come without a pedestal. He fixes it instead upon the pedestal formerly occupied by the 'old Apollo' and assures the general

[17] Marcus Tullius Cicero was known as 'Tully' in eighteenth-century Britain

that it now 'stands but half an inch lower than Diana'.

As well as this careful placing and pairing, White arranged for artisans from London (Lovell the painter, Johnson the carpenter and Pearson the plasterer) to repair damage incurred during transit, such as the 'bruising' on the arm of the smaller *Antinous* and a handle that had come off an urn. He reports that Pearson says he can repair it and is to 'bring a munday Morning a proper cement for that purpose ...' (13 March 1740). There is also the matter of painting the statues. John Cheere usually painted his work white before it left the yard, presumably both to simulate marble and to make it stand out against the green of the garden, as well as to preserve it from verdigris. He also painted some of his work in more lifelike colours (Davis 1991), perhaps in flesh colour or, especially in the case of the indoor pieces that would be viewed more closely, with more detailed marbling.

White mentions both these methods in the letters.[18] The two 'Great Bustos' on either side of the chimney piece are painted white (27 November 1740) and at the height of winter the Venus is brought indoors to the hall so that Lovell can give her several coats of white paint and allow them to dry before she is put back in 'Ye place from which she came' (24 December 1740). 'Proper collours for painting the Busto, Lovell brings along with him next Monday' (15 March 1739). Behind these detailed reassurances one can feel the general's meticulous, controlling will and the inadvisability of crossing it.

Two large sculptural pieces remain: *The Lion and the Horse and the Dying Gaul.* Both are known to have been ordered from Scheemakers by the general himself (Mowl 2007, p. 240). Both have strong associations with Rome, particularly with the Colosseum, where wild and domesticated animals as well as humans fought

[18] Moggridge states that some of the statues may have been painted bright yellow.

Il monumento equestre di Marco

each other to the death. Their size, their costliness,[19] the fame of their Roman originals and their prominent positions at the two chief viewing points across the river all suggest that they were the pride of the general's collection and of particular significance to him.

The Roman model for *The Lion and the Horse* is thought to be a copy of a fragment from a colossal Hellenistic group (now lost) with its origins in Pergamon in Asia Minor. Throughout the Dark Ages it was the only statue left standing on the Capitoline Hill, beside the flight of steps leading from the Palazzo Senatore.[20] From beside it, sentences of death were proclaimed and, by association, the lion was thought to represent the fell descent of law upon the wrongdoer. The steps became known as the *'scale della guistizia'* or simply, the *'scale al leone'*.

By then the statue was badly damaged. The horse's head was gone and to an ordinary eye the whole might have seemed little more than a lump of stone, revered mainly for its ancient associations. Yet Michelangelo, who famously claimed of his own works that he could see through lumps of stone to the statue within, 'judged it to be the most marvellous [meravigliosissio]' of all antique sculpture (Aldrovandi 1556, p. 251). When, in the late 1540s, he reconstructed the Capitoline, he had it transferred to the north-east side of the piazza. In 1594 it was restored by Bescape, who replaced the missing head. The whole was subsequently removed to the Palazzo Conservatori where it now forms part of a fountain in the museum garden.

Scheemakers gives the horse's head an agonized backward twist. Both he and Kent could have seen a similar version of the statue, in the garden of the Villa

[19] White recollects the price of the Gladiator as being £80, as compared to an average cost of the other full-length statues of about £20 (1743 inventory)

[20] It was mentioned in medieval mirabile as early as 1346 (Bober p. 176, as cited by Haskell and Penny 1981, p. 250, fn. 1).

The sculpture of 'The Lion and the Horse' left of the centre of the panorama of ancient Rome in the gardens of the Villa d'Este, by Giovanni Venturini. Metropolitan Museum of Art, New York. Photo Wikimedia Commons (detail)

d'Este where it had been placed in 1607 as a part of the 'Fountain of Rome'. An engraving by Venturini shows it on a raised panoramic model of the city. It stands on one side of the goddess Roma. On the other is a version of the she-wolf suckling Romulus and Remus. In this context the lion was seen both as one of the iconic images of the city and as representing Rome's repressive dominance over Tivoli; a dominance which the town's new prosperity and good governance under the d'Este family would, by inference, redress (Coffin 1960, p. 27).

At Rousham the statue is given particular prominence. It is placed on the central axial line of house and garden that runs from the entrance through the hall and out of the opposite door onto the north porch. From there it dissects the Bowling Green and continues to the triumphal arch on the far side of the river. The statue stands where this line intersects the far boundary of the Bowling Green and so dominates the visitor's first sight of the garden from the house and draws him or her forward towards a first view of the river.[21] Opinions differ as to its significance in this setting. Mowl sees The Lion as making a defining statement: 'a bitter comment on

[21] Letter from Clary dated 1750, quoted by Batey (1983).

life as he [the general], the battle hardened, had experienced the violence and the pain' (Mowl 2007, p. 240)

Clary, who shows little interest or awareness of any associations with the statues he so carefully lists, is nevertheless sensitive to their function in the landscape. He writes:

> 'When you walk out of at the Hall Door, [you see] two Minervas upon Terms [sic] … and in the middle stands a Lion devouring a Horse, upon a very Large pedestal, you walk forward to view the Lion nearer, when your eye drops upon a very fine Concave Slope, at the Bottom of which runs the Beautifull River Charvell and at the top stands two pretty Garden Seats,[22] one on each side, backt with the two Hilloks of Scotch Firrs, here you sit down first in the one, and then in the other, from whence perhaps at this time you have the prettiest view in the whole world' (Clary, cited in Batey 1983, p. 127).

Although, as Clary says, the visitor is drawn 'forward to view the Lion nearer', this does not seem to be in order to appreciate it as a piece of sculpture. The circling energies of its composition suggest the piece was designed to be seen in the round although the sharp descent of the Grand Slope on its north side makes it difficult, indeed hazardous, to do so. The Lion seems sited solely to guide visitors' steps and line of vision towards the countryside beyond at the same time that the slope prevents any comfortable attempt to proceed forward.

In fact the two *Hermathenae* mentioned by Clary may provide an answer. They mark the entrances to two paths, otherwise invisible, leading east and west down to the river. One of the heads is the familiar, helmeted image of the warlike Athena, the other is that of a smiling woman, only identifiable as the same goddess by the owl

[22] These are the two lattice-work kiosks designed by Kent and still in position at either end of the Bowling Green balustrade.

and olive branch carved on her plinth. The herms themselves are now overgrown and can easily go unnoticed, but a photograph of 1946 shows them arranged on either side of the Lion so as to form another group of three. Gordon (1999) suggests that together they confront the visitor with a moral choice as to whether to follow the smiling Athena, pointing the way to a life of ease and pleasure (i.e. Bridgeman's Theatre), or the armoured Athena directing the wanderer on a path of military duty ending in suffering and death, as represented by the Dying Gaul.

This final statue, known in the general's day as the *Dying Gladiator*, is a Portland stone version, carved by Scheemakers, of a fine Roman marble in the Capitoline Museum. The Roman statue, in its turn, is believed to be a copy of a bronze original made by a Greek sculptor from Pergamon in Asia Minor.[23] Modern recognition of the accurate ethnic detail – the warrior's shaven cheeks, his torque, his trumpet and the way in which the sculptor portrays his hair, dried into upright tufts by the application of limewash – has led to his more exact identification as a Galatian chieftain dying on the battlefield. The statue's history is complex: a long sequence

[23] Possibly Epigonus (Pliny, Natural History, XXXIV, 19).

of loss and reappearance, clues and supposition, much of it fiercely disputed.

The earliest reference to the piece is thought to be that of Pliny, who records the incident of a statue, which he calls 'The Trumpeter', being blown over in the Forum during a violent storm of wind. Because a curved trumpet is carved in bas-relief on the base of the marble Capitoline *Gladiator*, and because the wind was able to blow the statue so far, this is thought to be the lighter bronze original, brought from Pergamon to Rome *circa* 64 CE by Nero to decorate his *Domus Aurea* (Pliny, XXXIV, 84). The number of marble copies excavated in Rome indicate that, interpreted as a physically powerful enemy defeated by a Roman soldier, the statue was predictably popular at the time of Caesar's Gallic wars (Ridgway 1984, p. 23).

After that, all trace of either original or copies were lost for sixteen centuries under the vast wreckage of Rome

Then in 1623, a marble version of the statue reappeared. An entry in the Ludovisi inventories records 'A Gladiator of marble measuring some 10 palms' and again, ten years later, 'an ancient statue of a wounded gladiator larger than life, ...with a horn and shield nearby'. Its new owner, Ludovico Ludovisi, had seized the opportunity of the brief papacy (1621–23) of his uncle Gregory XV to increase the family's wealth and establish its status in Roman society. To do so, he bought property between the Pincian and the Quirinal hills on what was once the site of a famous garden belonging to the historian Sallust. This has raised the possibility that Julius Caesar, a previous tenant of the Horti Sallustiani, may, at one time, have owned the original statue and commissioned the subsequent copies.

When Ludovico embarked on building a grand villa on the site with a garden of its own, an essential part of that grandeur was the display of antique sculptures acquired in 1623, when he bought up the famous collection belonging to the Cesi family: his inventory for that year records details of purchase of one hundred sculptures from that single source. The fact that no such details were recorded for either the Gladiator or for another statue, known as *'The Suicide of the Gaul'* and thought by some to be its companion piece, suggests that no sale took place; that instead both were found on Ludovisi property when the foundations for the new villa were being dug. The artistic importance of the *Gladiator* was recognized immediately. By 1670 Giambattista Ludovisi considered it the most valuable single figure in his collection and estimated its worth as being twice that of any other piece.

No further light was thrown on the history of the statue until the German engineer Carl Humman began his excavation of Pergamon in 1878. There, on the forecourt of the temple of Athene Nikephorous, two plinths were found, one circular and one rectangular. They appear to form the bases for two separate sculptural groups dedicated to the goddess by Attilos I, as a thank-offering for his victory over the incursions of migrating Galatians. It has been suggested that the circular base was the plinth for the original bronze group comprising both the Ludovisi Gauls.

In an imaginative reconstruction of the entire work, the standing figure of 'The Suicide' twists around in mid-flight to face his pursuers. The energy of the figure spirals upward in a gesture that is both defiant and the epitome of defeat. He brandishes his sword above his head only to reverse it and plunge it fatally inside his collar bone and ribs. His wife, slain by his own hand, hangs limply from his free arm, One comrade, the 'Gladiator', crouches dying at his feet. The discarded sword and trumpet on the ground beside him suggest that the battle is over; that even if he could summons strength to blow the trumpet, there would be no one left to rally to him. Another Gaul lies dead across the base of the group and gives the composition visual stability. In this single tragic episode, the entire battlefield, indeed the fate of a whole tribe, is focused onto a single moment that encapsulates the whole event and effectively confronts the viewer with the human cost of victory.

Much as it might have pleased General Dormer that he and Julius Caesar had made the same choice of statue, he could have known nothing of its ancient history when Kent began work at Rousham in 1738. However, the single figure of the *Gladiator* was already well known in England and would have been familiar to him, at least from engravings, before Scheemakers put his new collection on view in London and advertised it in his catalogue. As early as 1644 John Evelyn had stated that the Gladiator was 'so much followed by all the rare artists as the many Copies and Statues testify, dispers'd through almost all Europ, both in stone & metall' (Evelyn,

4 November 1644).

By 1737 the statue had been acquired for the Capitoline Museum by Pope Clement XII where it was displayed to the public and regularly visited by 'Grand Tourists'. It was there that Scheemakers modelled it, by eye, in terracotta. An engraving by Bottari from *Del Museo Capitolino* (1741–82, vol. 3, p. 1, as cited by Haskell and Penny 1981, p. 225) shows a group of young artists eagerly sketching the *'Gladiator'* and a sculptor making a slightly less than life-size model in clay.

After Rome fell to Napoleon, the Capitoline *Gladiator* was among the famous ancient statues ceded to the French under the Treaty of Tolentino. It reached Paris in July 1798 in a triumphal procession of captured works of art and, while on display in the Louvre until its return to the Capitoline in the first half of 1816, it became accessible to a wider social range of British tourists and even better known.

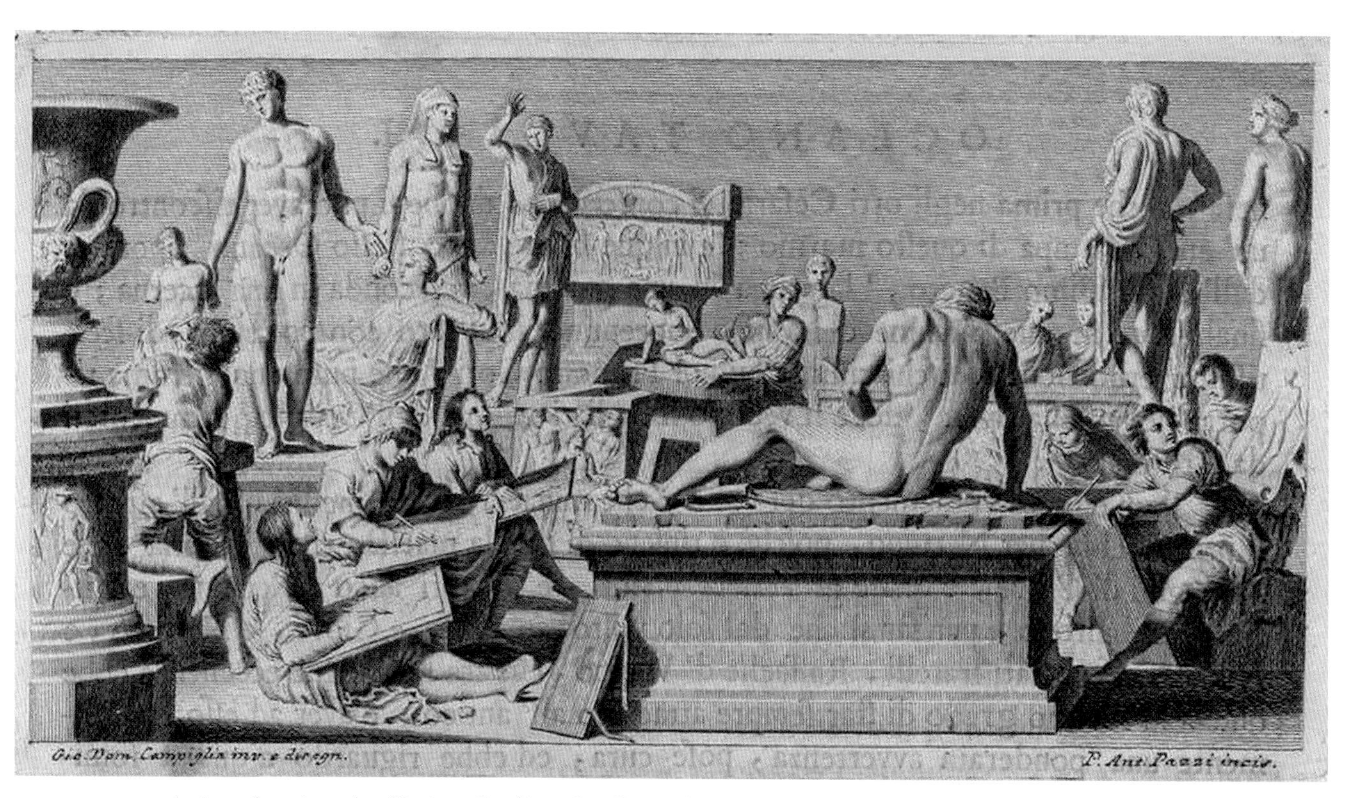

Artists drawing the 'Dying Gaul' at the Capitoline Museum, by Giovanni Domenico Campiglia, 1755.
© Alamy stock photo

Although Gunnis cites the Rousham copy as the first full-length version to be brought to England, by the end of the eighteenth century a few costly bronze and marble copies made in Rome were given pride of place in private collections: in marble, by Vierpy, at Wilton House for Lord Pembroke (Gunnis 1934, p. 410) and by Valadier for the Great Hall at the Duke of Northumberland's Syon House. The Royal Academy's plaster copy, cast from nineteenth-century moulds, was displayed to the public in Somerset House in the room where it stands today. Scheemakers' version

is a poor thing compared to the beautifully restored Roman copy in the Capitoline. By omitting the trumpet from the base and the torque from the man's neck, and by replacing the long battle sword with the shorter, two-sided gladiatorial sword he makes a more generalized figure, possibly representing a Gaul or possibly a Dacian, dying not on the battlefield but in the Roman arena. Like the *Lion* it is carved from Portland stone, a kind of limestone which is not entirely weatherproof and after even a few years in so exposed a position is bound to lose its outer layer, leaving a shallowly pitted surface. The absence of a polished surface is more profound than it might seem: Goethe wrote: 'Marble is an extraordinary material. Because of it the Apollo Belvedere gives such enormous pleasure. The bloom of eternal youth which the original statue possesses is lost even in the best plaster cast' (Goethe 1970, p. 152). The loss is particularly great in the case of the Gladiator where the poignancy of the figure lies in the fact that this is no immortal god, but a dying man from whom the bloom of mortal youth must rapidly fade. Above all the marble's fine rendering of facial expression is blurred.

Altogether it seems unlikely that the general chose the statue for aesthetic reasons alone. Indeed, its quality as a piece of sculpture seems not really to be at issue here. In his Unconnected Thoughts on Gardening (1765) William Shenston observes:

> 'A statue in a room challenges examination and is to be examined critically as a statue. A statue in a garden is to be considered as one part of a scene or landskip: the minuter touches are no more essential to it than a good landskip painter would esteem them were he to represent a statue in his picture' (as cited by Davis 1991, p. 27).

Reasons for its choice can only be guessed at. It seems likely that one was its instant recognizability from whatever angle it was seen, the elegant curve of the spine of the Gladiator being perhaps its most striking feature. By displaying it the general declared his intellectual identity with Republican Rome and his adherence to its strict moral code. At the same time its presence in his garden makes a silent statement, consistent with the ideals of the Kit-Cat Club, that eminence in the arts, refinement of taste, or being well versed in the classical writers, might put a man on equal footing with those of far greater wealth and social status.

There may also have been a more personal statement behind the general's choice. The herms which mark either end of the balustrade on the Praeneste roof are of

Hercules and Pan. Hercules is identified by his club and lion skin; Pan, in contrast to Nost's vigorous hybrid in the Vale, is entirely humanized.[24] A broad-brimmed shepherd's hat is pulled down over his animal ears and horns; his tail and hooves are hidden by a long shepherd's cloak. The herms too are now overgrown and difficult to see in their entirety but another photograph in Christopher Hussey's 1946 article shows them as part of an architectural grouping of three (Hussey 1946).

Again, Gordon (1999) interprets the two herms as offering different moral routes:

[24] The statue is thought to be based on that of the Good Shepherd in the Tribuna of the Uffizi.

Pan's to a life of pastoral retirement; Hercules' to a life of laborious duty. She interprets this as a specific reference to the general's choice to follow the dangers and hardships of the military life in preference to a life of retirement on his estates and refers to an inscription on the Triumphal Arch facing the Gladiator across the river:

> A gallant youth ('tis Lichfield's line)
> To Spain's proud capital shall wend his way
> And hear some cringing Don rehearse,
> Here England faught, and there yon portal stands
> The monument of Spain and valient Dormer's hands.
> (as cited by Gordon 1999, p. 84)

The combined group of the Gladiator and the herms could lend themselves to another reading. As the sixth son in a family with a strong military tradition, James Dormer would have had a strictly limited choice of career. He could not, in his youth, have expected to inherit, nor ever to be in a position to devote himself solely to his land. Even as the possibility came closer, his duty would still have been divided between the care of his estates and the defence of his country in time of war. The man to emulate would be the man who successfully combined both roles and excelled at both. Hercules and Pan could be said to represent the extremes of such a life, and the dying soldier placed between them that ideal of the Roman Republic: the farmer prepared at a moment's notice to leave his land and take up arms in defence of his neighbours' or his country's freedom. It is a figure with which the general might well have wished to identify.

Undoubtedly though, the Gladiator's chief attraction has always been its emotive power. Byron's response to it, written forty years after the general's death, is well known. He sees the Gladiator as portraying a victim of Roman power and brutality; a Dacian warrior, taken while defending his homeland and brought captive to Rome, perhaps one of the ten thousand gladiators forced to fight to the death in celebration of Trajan's victories of 107 CE (Dio 68.15, as cited by Grant 1967, p. 36).

In canto IV of Childe Harold's Pilgrimage, Byron's protagonist reaches Rome. By now Byron speaks as himself, a young aristocrat on his Grand Tour through a contemporary Europe. Vivid in his mind is the magnificent city of his school books, but what he finds is its vast owl-haunted ruins: 'a skeleton of her titanic form … a marble wilderness'. He admits to having little sympathy with sculpture: '… I have been accustomed to entwine/ My thoughts with nature rather in the fields' (IV, stanza LXI) rather than with art in galleries.

Nevertheless he does the rounds of the city's sculptural treasures: the *Laocoön*, the *Apollo Belvedere* and the *Dying Gladiator*. The first two he describes where they are displayed in the Vatican. There he assumes the voice of the tour guide: 'Or, turning to the Vatican go see/ Laocoön's torture dignifying pain …/ Or view the Lord of the unerring bow …' (stanzas CLX and CLXI). They are works of art: their context is the gallery. His reaction to the *Gladiator* is different; he does not describe it as a part of his visit to the Capitoline. Indeed, he never does describe it as a piece of sculpture. Instead he allows his imagination to play on what it represents and makes that a visionary episode in his visit to the Colosseum itself: 'I see before me the Gladiator lie:/ He leans upon his hand – his manly brow/ Consents to death but conquers agony' (stanza CXL). He responds to what the sculptor has made implicit in the statue: the dying man's stoicism, the inward concentration of his features, his protracted final moments:

'… his droop'd head sinks gradually low
And through his side the last drops, ebbing slow
From the red gash, fall heavy, one by one
Like the first of a thunder shower …'
(stanza CXL)

Poetry frees Byron to travel beyond what the bodily eye can see. In Lessing's words (1930), he sees 'not with the eye but with the eye of the imagination and with that is able to live the experience of the *Gladiator*':

'The arena swims around him – he is gone,
Ere ceased the inhuman shout which hailed the wretch who won.
He heard it, but he heeded not – his eyes
Were with his heart, and that was far away;
He reek'd not of the life he lost nor prize
But where his rude hut by the Danube lay,
There were his young barbarians all at play,
There was their Dacian mother – he their sire,

Butchered to make a Roman holiday ...'

(stanzas CXL and CXLI)

There is no record of James Dormer's response to the statue. He appears to have been drawn to both the *Gladiator* and the *Lion* by the very subjects whose grimness makes them seem curious choices today. In the past the display of such memento mori in a garden was not unusual. Nearly two centuries before James Dormer inherited Rousham, another soldier, Vicino, Duke of Orsini, filled his garden at Bomarzo with grotesque and terrifying forms: a series of hell-mouths, carved into natural outcrops of tufa. Among them he inscribed many quotations including the quoted phrase, 'For the relief of the heart'. The general left no such verbal clues, but it may well be that both men felt a need to give some expression to the recurring images of cruelty and suffering they had witnessed on the battlefield. Perhaps the general felt that the beauty of Rousham might in some way absorb the pain of such images and, in doing so, heal his own. Perhaps he wished to acknowledge the brothers with whom he must have played in this garden domain and whose deaths enabled him to inherit it. Perhaps he felt the need to contemplate his own approaching end. A sketch of the Gladiator by Kent, with a sarcophagus as its base, suggests that it may have been considered as a memorial to the general, but as it is without caption or date, this can only be speculation.

Two things are certain: that the subject of both these large statues is not Death in the abstract, but the moments preceding it and how they are experienced (by the horse, in terror; by the man, with stoical dignity) and that the general himself was dying. From the start of the innovations his health had been poor. As early as 1738 Kent had written to Pope that the general 'although crippled by a regular fit of gout' was still 'bronzo mad' (Sherburn 1956, p. 188). White reports that preparations for the reception of *The Lion and the Horse and the Gladiator* are nearly complete: 'The pedestal over ye Arcade … is in hand and may be work't in a fortnight's time. That in the parterre will be set up today' but only eight days later, White breaks off in the middle of a letter to the general at Bath, where the latter had been taking the waters: 'Sorry am I to hear of your relapse' (23 November 1740). A servant has been sent by the Oxford coach to help him. He reverts quickly to the happier subject of

Sketch for a sarcophagus with the 'Dying Gaul', by William Kent, c. 1739. © The Devonshire Collections, Chatsworth. Reproduced by permission of Chatsworth Settlement Trustees

the placing of busts in the Praeneste.

In December, advance preparations for the summer visit contain hints that the general's world is closing in and that he can no longer reach the remoter parts of his garden. Clary writes to Sir Clement that the ground to the right of the Grand Slope is prepared, 'which Mr. Kent desires planted with flowering shrubs that the General may have a view over them to Heyford from the porch' (Clary to Sir Clement Cottrell, 15 February 1741). The shifting of Kent's two latticed kiosks from the end of the Bowling Green to six feet (2m) nearer the house and the raising of the ground where he plans to put them by three feet (1m), so that they are level with the terrace and command a better view, may show the same concern.

By July there is an increased sense of frustration at Kent's delays and a new urgency that all the garden statues should be in place before the general leaves for London. Dormer himself writes to Sir Clement Cottrell:

> 'According to your promise this comes to summons you to Rousham, I am now left alone & the sooner You do me the pleasure the more agreable to me will be. I hope Ld Burlington does not forget his word. & if Kent can be persuaded to come I shall take it very kindly ... Be so kind as to call at Scheemakers' and quicken him, I am still in hopes that he will be here by the end of August to set up the statue before the Weather proves bad. I am, dear Clement/ Yours J. Dormer' (General Dormer to Sir Clement Cottrell, 21 July 1741, cited by Müller 1997, p. 187).

The letter is preserved in the family archive with a note on the back in Sir Clement's hand: 'The poor dear general's last letter to me' (Gordon 1999, p. 64).

In fact one more survives. On 22 September, Dormer writes in apparent good spirits, thanking his cousin for his help in negotiating for bronzes and statutes

through an agent in London and planning to be in town 'presently after Michaelmas as I always intended'. He goes on to congratulate Sir Clement on the birth of a second son and signs the letter, 'I am with great truth Dear Sr Clement/ Your most faithful kinsman and humble Serv J. Dormer' (Müller 1997, p. 187).

By 1 December, White writes from Rousham that the general's condition has worsened. He has been in Bath again, taking the waters, but they have

> '… disagree'd with him, he has been forc'd to leave them quite off, & continues so weak, as to not be in a Condition of bearing ye Jolts of an hir'd Coach; His Berlin [a large travelling coach in which the General could lie out] & horses are therefor'd order'd to be at Bath ye 9th Instant, purposing to Sett out for London ye Eleventh …' (*ibid.*).

White, without question his faithful friend as well as his servant, plans to meet him there 'if nothing material happens'.

That meeting may never have taken place. James Dormer died on Christmas Eve of 1741, at Crendon (now Grendon Underwood) in Buckinghamshire, and was buried there on 2 January 1742. He had lived to see Sir Clement's two sons secure the inheritance and would have known that they were to add the name of Dormer to their own. He had seen his dream of Rousham realized, its house extended, its garden transformed, his statues set in their chosen places, an expression of himself and his allotted role in life for us to read as best we can.

The garden had become, in those last lonely months. a place where the general could contemplate how, in spite of pain, he might achieve the good death that confirmed a man's worth. There is no trace of Christian symbolism at Rousham among the pagan gods. The general may well have turned instead to Cicero for his stern Roman brand of consolation. He would have been surprised to find that his ancient 'schoolmaster' was by now only a few years older than himself. Cicero was 63 when he wrote his *Tusculan Disputations* (completed in BCE 44) on the subject of old age and death. His bitter public criticisms of Mark Antony had led the great advocate into disfavour. He had left Rome and prolonged his annual summer visit to his properties along the coast of the Campania, moving from one to another in daily expectation of death at the hands of Antony's followers. In this plight he contemplates death steadily, even cheerfully. He can still find delight in the study of Greek literature and the close observation of growing things. 'Nothing can either furnish necessaries more richly and present a fairer spectacle, than well cultivated land. And to the enjoyment of that, old age does not merely present no hindrance – it actually invites and allures to it' (Cicero 1927, 16, p. 82). As for death, he says it is a 'lesson which must be studied from our youth, for unless that is learnt, no-one can have a quiet mind. For die we certainly must, and that too without being certain whether it may not be this very day' (*ibid.*, 20).

Paradoxically Cicero choses the despised and defeated gladiator as a model for how death should be met: 'What gladiator, of even moderate reputation, ever gave a sigh? who ever turned pale? who ever disgraced himself either in the actual combat, or even when about to die? who that had been defeated ever drew in his neck to avoid the stroke of death?' (Cicero 1877, Book II, XVII). Only months later, when his political enemies caught up with him, Cicero kept to his own precepts. In Plutarch's account, he heard his murderers coming and

> '... ordered his servants to set the litter down where they were. He himself, in that characteristic posture of his, with his chin resting on his left hand, looked steadfastly at his murderers. He was all covered in dust; his hair was long and disordered, and his face was pinched and wasted with his anxieties – so that most of those who stood by covered their faces while Herennius was killing him' (Plutarch 1981, 48, 3–5).

Even in that plight, Cicero copied the gladiator's gesture of fearless compliance in his own death. 'His throat was cut,' Plutarch writes, 'as he stretched out his neck from the litter' (*ibid.*).

No contemporary epitaph exists at Rousham for James Dormer, but an epitaph on

Robert Dormer (attributed to Pope) contains the resounding couplet: 'Dauntless he saw grim death appear,/ Who ever knew a Dormer fear'. There can be little doubt that the general followed his brother's example with courage and resolution.

In 1764, after the deaths of the general and Sir Clement, the latter's heir, Charles Cottrell-Dormer, put up the general's books for auction and redecorated the denuded library in the then fashionable rococo style, retaining only Kent's ceiling and chimneypiece and his brackets to support the collection of bronzes. As if to make amends, the general's portrait, painted by van Loo on his accession to Rousham in 1738, was brought down from London and hung above the chimneypiece. It shows a man alert, but approachable, wearing a scarlet coat. In the broken pediment above his head there is a bust of Cicero. The two portraits together seem to form an indoor memorial, as the Gladiator does an outdoor one.

The Grand Parlour (formerly General Dormer's library) showing the general's portrait over the fireplace with a bust of Cicero above it. Courtesy of a private collection.

Bibliography

Aldrovandi, Ulisse, *Della statue antiche che per tutta Roma in divers luoghi* ... in Mauro Lucio, *Le antichita de la città di Roma*, Rome, 1556.

Barton, Carlin A. *The Sorrows of the Ancient Romans: The Gladiator and the Monster*, Princeton University Press, Princeton NJ, 1993.

Batey, Mavis, 'The Way to View Rousham by Kent's Gardener', *Garden History*, vol. 11, no. 2 (Autumn 1983), pp. 125–132.

Blackett-Ord, Carol, 'Letters from William Kent to Burrell Massingberd from the Continent, 1712–1719', *The Volume of the Walpole Society*, vol. 63 (2001), pp. 75–109.

Byron, George Gordon, Lord, *Poetical Works,* Oxford University Press, London, 1952.

Chase, Isabel (ed.), *Horace Walpole, Gardenist*, Princeton University Press, Princeton NJ, 1943.

Cicero, Marcus Tullius, 'On Bearing Pain,' Book II in *Tusculan Disputations* (trans. C.D. Yonge), Harper & Brothers, New York, 1877. Available online at gutenberg.org

Cicero, Marcus Tullius, 'On Friendship', from T*wo Essays on Old Age and Friendship* (trans. E.S. Shuckburgh), Macmillan, London, 1927.

Coffin, David R., *The Villa D'Este at Tivoli*, Princeton University Press, Princeton NJ, 1960.

Coffin, David R., 'The Elysian Fields of Rousham', *Proceedings of the American Philosophical Society*, vol. 130, no. 4 (December 1986), pp. 406–423.

Cottrell-Dormer, Frances, *Account of Rousham, Oxfordshire,* by F.E.C.D., Nabu, Charleston SC, 2012.

Davis, John, *Antique Garden Ornament*, Antique Collectors' Club, Woodbridge, 1991.

Dettiene, Marcel, *Dionysos Slain* (trans. Mireille Muellner and Leonard Muellner), Johns Hopkins University Press, Baltimore, 1979.

Evelyn, John, *The Diary of John Evelyn*, vol. 1. Available online with commentary by Richard Garnett at gutenberg.org

Goethe, Johann Wolfgang von, *Italian Journey*, 1786–1788 (trans. W.H. Auden and Elizabeth Mayer), Penguin, Harmondsworth, 1970.

Gordon, Susan, 'The Iconography and Mythology of the Eighteenth-Century Landscape Garden', unpubl. PhD thesis, University of Bristol, 1999.

Gunnis, Rupert, *Dictionary of British Sculptors*, 1660–1851, Harvard University Press, Cambridge MA, 1934.

Grant, Michael, *Gladiators*, Delacorte Press, New York, 1967.

Haskell, Francis, and Penny, Nicholas, *Taste and the Antique: The Lure of Classical Sculpture*, 1500–1900, Yale University Press, New Haven CT and London, 1981.

Hartswick, Kim J., *The Gardens of Sallust*: A Changing Landscape, University of Texas Press, Austin TX, 2004.

HMC (Historical Monuments Commission), Letter of Sir Thomas Robinson, in *The Manuscripts of the Earl of Carlisle ...*,

15th Report, Appendix part VI, HMSO, London, 1897.

Hölscher, Tonio, *The Language of Images in Roman Art* (trans. Annemarie Kunzl-Snodgrass), Cambridge University Press, Cambridge, 2004. Orig. publ. in German as *Romanische Bildsprache als semantisches System*, Heidelberg, 1987.

Hopkins, Keith, *Death and Renewal*, Cambridge University Press, Cambridge, 1983.

Hunt, John Dixon, William Kent: *Landscape Garden Designer*, Zwemmer, London, 1987.

Hunt, John Dixon, *Gardens and the Picturesque: Studies in the History of Garden Architecture*, MIT Press, Cambridge MA and London, 1992.

Hunt, John Dixon, and Willis, Peter, *The Genius of the Place: The English Landscape Garden, 1620–1820*, MIT Press, Cambridge MA, 1988.

Hussey, Christopher, 'A Georgian Arcady: I', *Country Life*, vol. 99, no. 2578 (14 June 1946), pp. 1084–1087.

Ingamells, John, *A Dictionary of British and Irish Travellers in Italy, 1701–1800*, Yale University Press, New Haven CT, 1997.

Jourdain, Margaret, *The Work of William Kent: Artist, Painter, Designer and Landscape Gardener,* Country Life, London, 1948.

Langley, Batty, *New Principles of Gardening*, Bettesworth & Batley, London, 1728. Available online at books.google.com

Lessing, Gotthold, *Laocoön* (trans. and intro. William A. Steel), Everyman, London, 1930. Orig. publ. 1766.

Livy, *Rome and Italy* (trans. Betty Radice), Books VI–X of The History of Rome, Penguin Classics, London, 1982.

Marvin, Miranda, *The Language of the Muses,* J. Paul Getty Museum, Los Angeles, 2008.

McDayter, Mark: 'Poetic Gardens and Political Myths: The Renewal of St. James's Park in the Restoration', *Journal of Garden History*, vol. 15, no. 3 (Autumn 1995), pp. 135–148.

Moggridge, Hal, 'Kent's Garden at Rousham', *Journal of Garden History*, vol. 6, no. 3 (1982), pp. 187–226.

Mowl, Timothy, *William Kent: Architect, Designer, Opportunist*, Random House, London, 2007.

Müller, Ulrich, 'Rousham: A Transcription of the Steward's Letters, 1734–42', Garden History, vol. 25, no. 2 (Winter 1997), pp. 178–188.

Nichols, John, *Literary Anecdotes of the Eighteenth Century*, 6 vols, Nichols, Son & Bentley, London, 1812–16.

Pepys, Samuel, *The Diary of Samuel Pepys, 1660,* ed. Robert Latham and William Matthews, Harper Collins, London, 1995. Available online at books.google.com

OCCL (Oxford Companion to Classical Literature), ed. M.C. Howatson, Oxford University Press, Oxford, 1997.

ODNB (Oxford Dictionary of National Biography), Oxford University Press, Oxford, 2004.

Phibbs, John, 'The Structure of the Eighteenth-Century Garden', *Journal of the Garden History Society*, vol. 38, no. 1 (Summer 2010), pp. 20–34.

Pliny the Elder, *Natural History: A Selection,* intro. and trans. John F. Healy, Penguin Classics, London, 1991 repr. 2004.

Plutarch, 'Cicero', in *Fall of the Roman Republic* (trans. Rex Warner), Penguin, Harmondsworth, 1981.

Pollitt, Jerome Jordan, *The Art of Rome c. 753 BC–AD 337: Sources and Documents,* Cambridge University Press, Cambridge, 1983.

Pope, Alexander, *Moral Essays, Epistle IV, to Richard Boyle, Earl of Burlington*, ed. Bonamy Dobrée, Dent, London, 1969.

Ralph, James, *A Critical Review of the Public Buildings, Statues and Ornaments in and about London and Westminster*, London, 1734. Available online at books. google.com

Richardson, Tim, *The Arcadian Friends: Inventing the English Landscape Garden*, Bantam, London, 2007.

Ridgway, B.S., *Roman Copies of Greek Sculptures*, Jerome Lectures series, University of Michigan Press, Ann Arbor, 1984.

Ritchie, W.F., and Ritchie, J.N.G., *Celtic Warriors*, Shire Publications, Princes Risborough, 1985.

Roscoe, Ingrid, 'Peter Scheemakers (1691–1781)', *The Volume of the Walpole Society*, vol. 61 (1999), pp. 163–304.

Sheeler, Jessie, *The Garden at Bomarzo: A Renaissance Riddle*, Frances Lincoln, London, 2007.

Sherburn, George (ed.), *The Correspondence of Alexander Pope, Vol. 4: 1736–1744*, Oxford University Press, Oxford, 1956.

Suffolk, Henrietta, Countess of, *Letters To and From Henrietta, Countess of Suffolk, and Her Second Husband, the Hon. George Berkeley, From 1712 to 1767*, vol. 2, John Murray, London, 1824.

Switzer, Stephen, *Ichnographia Rustica: Or the Nobleman, Gentleman, and Gardener's Recreation*, Garland, New York and London, 1982. Orig. publ. 1718.

Toynbee, Jocelyn, *Roman Portrait Busts*, Arts Council of Great Britain, London, 1953.

Walpole, Horace, *Essay on Modern Gardening*, facsimile of 1771 edn, printed Kirkgate Press, Canton PA, 1904. Available online at https://archive.org/details/essayonmodernga00walpgoog/page/n106/mode/2up

Vertue, George, *Note Books*. Vol. 3 (orig. publ. 1730) publ. in The Volume of the Walpole Society, vol. 22, 1935–36; Vol. 4 in The Volume of the Walpole Society, vol. 24, 1935–36. Available online at jstor.org

Walpole, Horace, *The History of the Modern Taste in Gardening*, pp. 25–29 in Isabel Chase (ed.), Horace Walpole, Gardenist, Princeton University Press, Princeton NJ, 1943.

Willis, Peter, 'From Desert to Eden: Charles Bridgeman's "Capital Stroke"', *Burlington Magazine*, vol. 115, no. 840 (March 1973), pp. 150–157.

Woodbridge, Kenneth, 'William Kent's Gardening: The Rousham Letters', *Apollo*, vol. 100 (1974), pp. 282–291.